*Y*OUR

REHEARSAL

*D*AY

Featuring The Best Selling

*W*EDDING *P*ARTY

RESPONSIBILITY

*C*ARDS

Christian and Jewish versions included

Published by Wedding Solutions

© Copyright 1999

Printed in China

ISBN 1-887169-07-5

DEDICATED TO:

Brides and grooms everywhere. May the months before your wedding be productive, fun and most of all, memorable.

*T*ABLE OF *C*ONTENTS

*I*NTRODUCTION

Congratulations on your engagement! Now it's time to get down to business. There's a lot of work ahead of you, but with the right planning tools, it can be much easier and less stressful than you might think.

Planning a wedding is a lot like putting on a play. There are the stars of the show, the bride and groom, and the supporting players, the wedding party. And just like a play, you need a rehearsal to ensure everything goes smoothly on opening night, or in this case, the Wedding Day.

Your Rehearsal Day is everything you need to know to plan a productive rehearsal day and, in turn, make for a memorable, stress-free wedding. Included are handy checklists to make sure you've taken care of every last detail, helpful tips on deciding who will be part of your wedding, where to hold the rehearsal and dinner, unique ideas and suggestions to make the dinner special, great gifts to give your wedding party, samples of invitations, unforgettable toasts, and much more!

As an added bonus, this book contains both Christian and Jewish versions of the best-selling *Wedding Party Responsibility Cards*. These useful cards contain all the information your wedding party needs to know to assure a smooth wedding: what to do, when to arrive, what to bring, as well as each member's position in the processional, recessional, and ceremony.

Cards are included for each member of the wedding party: the Maid of Honor, Best Man, 6 Bridesmaids, 6 Ushers, Parents of the Bride, Parents of the Groom, Flower Girl, Ring Bearer, and of course the Bride and Groom. These cards are perforated for easy removal and scored down the middle for ease in folding and mailing.

YOUR WEDDING PARTY

Determining who will be in your wedding party can be a difficult decision for many brides and grooms. You and your fiancé must consider several factors, including the number of guests attending, the location of the ceremony, and the budget. (Remember, you will be buying gifts and flowers for each member of the wedding party.)

While the number of attendants is up to you, traditionally the more formal the wedding, the more attendants. The general rule is one usher for every fifty guests. It is preferable that there be an equal number of bridesmaids and ushers because this looks better in pictures and ensures each bridesmaid has an escort down the aisle. But having a couple of extra bridesmaids or ushers should not be a problem as they can simply walk down the aisle together.

Most likely, you will choose family members and close friends to be your attendants. You should, however, consider several factors when deciding who to ask: Can they afford to purchase their own attire? Can they finance their own travel (if from out of town)? Are they comfortable around people? Can they handle the expected responsibilities?

The following are ideas and guidelines for choosing your wedding party. Their specific duties and responsibilities will be discussed later in the book.

$\mathcal{M}$AID OF HONOR

Your maid/matron of honor should obviously be someone very special to you. A maid of honor is single, and a matron of honor is married. This person is usually a sister, which can serve to alleviate a lot of worry in having to choose among several close friends. In the event you have more than one sister, typically the sister closest in age to the bride is chosen. If you find it difficult to choose, try a diplomatic system such as drawing straws; or in the case of several sisters, assign each sister to be another's maid of honor so that no one feels left out. The same can be done with a group of close girlfriends in case you do not have a sister and are worried about feelings getting hurt.

$\mathcal{B}$RIDESMAIDS

You will most likely choose your close friends and/or sisters to be your bridesmaids. Again, the number will depend on the size of the wedding, but you should never have more than twelve. The simpler the wedding, the less bridesmaids you should have.

The sister(s) of the groom is frequently included as a bridesmaid, but this is not obligatory, especially if the two of you have never met. That having been said, it is always a nice gesture to invite your future sister-in-law to be part of the wedding since you will likely be seeing each other on a regular basis at family gatherings.

If a friend or relative is obviously pregnant and feels uncomfortable being part of the wedding party, honor her wishes and choose someone else. However, if both of you are comfortable with it, by all means include her.

If you absolutely cannot decide between friends and/or relatives but do not want to exceed a certain number of bridesmaids, consider asking those special people to read a scripture, poem or other meaningful verse at the ceremony. If your friend has a talented voice, have them sing during the ceremony or even at the reception.

JUNIOR BRIDESMAID

If there is a young girl you would like to include as part of the wedding party who is too old to be a flower girl and too young to be a bridesmaid, you may consider making her a junior bridesmaid. She is not obligated to participate in the traditional bridesmaids' duties and need only be included in the procession. As such, she should walk at the end of the procession after the last bridesmaid. Her dress may match the other bridesmaids or may be altered to look more appropriate for her age. If there is a junior usher, he will escort her during the recessional.

FLOWER GIRL

The flower girl is usually between the ages of four and eight. It is not recommended that she be any younger than four since expecting such a young child to follow directions and stand still during the ceremony may backfire. Use your best judgment. Hopefully, you will know the child well enough to be familiar with her behavior and decide whether she would make a good choice.

The flower girl is often the daughter of a close friend or relative of the bride, but may also be a younger sister or relative of the groom. She will be the last one down the aisle before the bride. If she is on the younger side, you may want to have her walk down the aisle and then be seated with her parents before the ceremony begins. An older flower girl may stand behind the maid of honor during the ceremony and, along with the ring bearer (if there is one), follow the bride and groom during the recessional. Although she may attend the rehearsal, her parents should ensure she gets enough sleep the night before the wedding so she is not temperamental during her walk down the aisle or throughout the ceremony.

BEST MAN

The best man holds his title for a reason. Next to the bride and groom, he is the most important person in the wedding party. As the groom, you want to make sure he is someone who is not only close to you, but responsible as well. Normally a brother is chosen, but you may choose a close friend or even your father to hold this honor. As with the maid of honor, choosing a brother (if you have one) may relieve some of the stress of having to choose among a several friends.

Once chosen, make sure the best man understands all of his responsibilities. His overall job is to take care of as many of the groom's duties as possible. These duties are explained in detail in the *Wedding Party Responsibility Cards* contained at the end of this book.

*U*SHERS

When choosing ushers, you should follow the same basic guidelines as with the bridesmaids. Ushers are usually brothers or close friends of the groom. Their main duty is to seat guests before the ceremony and escort the bridesmaids.

If the bride has a brother, it is a nice gesture for the groom to include him. Again, this is a good way for future in-laws to get acquainted if they haven't yet done so.

It is helpful to appoint a head usher, preferably one who has ushered at previous weddings, to organize the other ushers and make sure that special guests are seated in their proper places. The head usher should *not* be the best man since the best man will be busy with many other details before, during, and after the ceremony.

*J*UNIOR USHER

If you have a young brother, cousin, etc., you may want to include him in the wedding party as a junior usher. He will not have to carry the same responsibilities as the other ushers, but will dress like them and participate in the procession. He will walk behind the other ushers in the processional. If there is a junior bridesmaid, he may escort her during the recessional.

*R*ING BEARER

The ring bearer is usually between the ages of four and eight. He should not be any younger than four. Expecting such a young child to hold still for any length of time is asking for trouble. If there will be a flower girl, it is preferable that they be close in age and get along fairly well since they will be walking together during the recessional.

The ring bearer is often the son of a close friend or relative, but he may also be a younger brother or relative of the bride or groom. The ring bearer will precede the flower girl down the aisle. If he is very young, he should walk down the aisle and then be seated with his parents before the ceremony begins. An older ring bearer may stand behind the best man during the ceremony. As with the flower girl, the ring bearer's parents are responsible for making sure he gets the proper amount of sleep to prevent any possible crankiness or misbehavior during his walk down the aisle or throughout the ceremony.

Wedding Party Form

(Make a copy of this form and give it to your wedding consultant)

Parents		Home No.	Work No.
Bride's Mother			
Bride's Father			
Groom's Mother			
Groom's Father			

Bride's Attendants		Home No.	Work No.
Maid of Honor			
Matron of Honor			
Bridesmaid			
Bridesmaid			
Bridesmaid			
Bridesmaid			
Bridesmaid			
Bridesmaid			
Junior Bridesmaid			
Flower Girl			
Other			

Groom's Attendants		Home No.	Work No.
Best Man			
Usher			
Usher			
Usher			
Usher			
Usher			
Usher			
Junior Usher			
Ring Bearer			
Other			

PRE-WEDDING PARTIES

A wedding is a great excuse to celebrate! Before the "Big Day" arrives, your family and friends may want to throw you a party or two. While you should be very grateful to these gracious hosts, make sure there are not so many parties that your friends and loved ones are left penniless when it comes to the actual wedding. It is also a good idea to make sure these parties are not too close to the wedding date as they may take away from critical planning time.

Invitations are always a nice touch to a celebration of any kind, although they are not required in every case. Usually invitations are only essential in formal occasions. If any of your pre-wedding parties fall into this category, it is proper to send invitations. If the parties are of a more casual nature, it is not necessary to send them but if you would like to, by all means, go ahead! Included within the description of each pre-wedding party are sample invitations, both formal and less formal. Also, see page 47 for a chart with guidelines on addressing invitations.

*E*NGAGEMENT PARTY

The purpose of the engagement party is to announce the couple's intentions to marry and introduce them to family and friends before the wedding. This party should take place within a reasonable period of time after the actual engagement. It is customarily given by the parents, but there are no set rules; a relative or close family friend is just as appropriate. The party may be a brunch, luncheon, dinner, or cocktail party. Invitations may be sent but are not required unless the party is formal. Usually the host or hostess will announce the newly engaged couple and wish them well with a toast. Gifts are not required, but a card or a bottle of champagne is a nice gesture.

Formal Invitation:

Mr. and Mrs. Charles Dawson
are pleased to announce the engagement of their daughter
Shelley Lynne
to
Mr. Bryan Thomas
and request your company at a party in their honor
on the 9th of January
at seven o'clock
9741 Birchwood Lane
Atlanta, Georgia 30350
RSVP (770) 555-3689

Less Formal:

You're invited to an engagement party
in honor of Shelley Dawson and Bryan Thomas
on January 9th at 7 PM
9741 Birchwood Lane
Given by: Kathy and Charles Dawson
RSVP (770) 555-3689

Engagement Party Worksheet

Type of Party: _____

Host/Hostess: _____

Phone #: _____

Date: _____

Time: _____

Location: _____

Expected No. of Guests: _____

	Description	**Estimated Cost**	**Actual Cost**
Food:			
Beverages:			
Rentals:			
Decorations:			

Total: $**_____   **$_____

NOTES: _____
_____
_____
_____

GUEST AND GIFT LIST

ENGAGEMENT PARTY

Name Telephone No. Street Address City, State, Zip Code	Rsvp How Many ?	Gift	Thank You Sent ✓

GUEST AND GIFT LIST
ENGAGEMENT PARTY

Name Telephone No. Street Address City, State, Zip Code	Rsvp How Many ?	Gift	Thank You Sent ✓

*B*RIDAL SHOWER

This party is usually given by an aunt, maid of honor, bridesmaid or family friend, but traditionally is not given by a member of your immediate family. If you are going to have more than one shower, make sure you talk to each hostess and set your dates well in advance to prevent any scheduling conflicts. Be sure not to invite the same friends to every shower, as they may tire of having to buy you several gifts as well as a wedding gift. Consider having a shower with just work friends, one with your closest friends, one with family, etc. Of course, this is all dependent on who is hosting. You should offer to help with the shower, but the hostess is ultimately in charge of who is invited, how many are invited, and what type of shower it will be.

TYPES OF SHOWERS: A bridal shower can have several themes. A "kitchen shower" would obviously call for gifts associated with the kitchen: mixing bowls, dish towels, cooking utensils, etc. You can also have a "lingerie shower" to help you get ready for your "Big Night" after the "Big Day"! Another fun theme is a "Time of Day" shower where every guest is assigned a certain time of day and brings something appropriate for that time. For example, 7 AM may bring towels, 12 PM might give a picnic basket, and 6 PM may call for cookware or beverage glasses.

Another shower which has increased in popularity is a "couples shower" where both the bride and groom are honored. The shower is co-ed and guests can either buy one gift for the couple or two smaller gifts, one for the bride and one for the groom. A barbecue or pool party might be a good idea for this type of shower since there may be more people, and the atmosphere will likely be more festive.

GAMES: Games are typically played at the shower, and small gifts are given as prizes. Try seeing how well your guests know you: think of 10-20 questions about yourself and see who knows the most answers, or have the hostess give everyone paper and pencils and have them draw what they think your wedding gown looks like. If you are having a couples shower, have the bride and groom answer 10-20 questions about each other, and have the guests bet on who will answer more correctly.

GIFTS: It is always a nice gesture to have favors for all the guests. Small tokens such as chocolates, candles, lotions, or simple picture frames are nice but inexpensive ideas for gifts.

Remember to send thank you notes as soon as possible for all your shower gifts. Your promptness is not only polite but will also lighten your load a bit since you will soon be writing many more thank you notes after your wedding gifts start flowing in.

Formal Invitation:

Mrs. Sharon Nelson
invites you to attend a bridal shower
in honor of
Miss Shelley Dawson
February twentieth at two o'clock
1248 Newbury Road
Atlanta, Georgia 30350
RSVP (770) 555-2721
Lingerie Shower

Less Formal:

You're Invited to a Bridal Shower!

For: Shelley Dawson
Date: February 20th
Time: 2:00 PM
Place: 1248 Newbury Road
Given by: Sharon Nelson
RSVP: (770) 555-2721
Lingerie theme

Since a bridal shower is a festive occasion, you may want to be creative and hand make invitations that correspond with the theme of your shower. For instance, if you are having a "Time of Day" shower, construct your invitations to look like clocks; and if you're really good, make little hands that point to the appropriate time of day you've assigned to that particular guest. Be inventive and make it fun!

*B*RIDAL *S*HOWER *W*ORKSHEET

Type of Party: _____

Host/Hostess: _____

Phone #: _____

Date: _____

Time: _____

Location: _____

Expected No. of Guests: _____

	Description	**Estimated Cost**	**Actual Cost**
Food:			
Beverages:			
Rentals:			
Decorations:			

Total: $_____ $_____

NOTES: _____

_____

_____

_____

Guest and Gift List
BRIDAL SHOWER

Name Telephone No. Street Address City, State, Zip Code	Rsvp How Many ?	Gift	Thank You Sent ✓
_____ _____ _____			
_____ _____ _____			
_____ _____ _____			
_____ _____ _____			
_____ _____ _____			
_____ _____ _____			

Guest and Gift List
BRIDAL SHOWER

Name Telephone No. Street Address City, State, Zip Code	Rsvp How Many ?	Gift	Thank You Sent ✓

*B*RIDESMAIDS' LUNCHEON

Since your bridesmaids have helped you throughout the tumultuous yet exciting months of wedding planning, a bridesmaids' luncheon is a great way to thank them for all their time and hard work. It can be given a few days before the wedding or on the day of the rehearsal, and can be hosted in a restaurant, a club, or your home. While this occasion is to honor your bridesmaids, other special guests such as mothers, grandmothers, or aunts may be invited. Other wedding party participants such as your reader, vocalist, or flower girl may also be included.

This is the time to present your bridesmaids with their gifts. It is also the time to thank your wedding party for all their planning skills and entertaining abilities. Thank your mother for her efforts, and any other guests you feel have gone out of their way to make your wedding special. While you may get a chance to toast all these individuals at the rehearsal dinner, this is a great way to single them out and thank each one of them personally.

Formal Invitation:

Miss Shelley Dawson
invites you to attend a luncheon
in honor of
her bridesmaids
Friday, March nineteenth at 12 noon
The Magnolia Inn
5700 Magnolia Way
Atlanta, Georgia 30350
RSVP
(770) 555-3689

Less Formal:

A Bridesmaids' Luncheon

For: The bridesmaids! (Carrie, Tara, Leslie, Amy, and Diane)
Date: March 19th
Time: 12:00 PM
Place: The Magnolia Inn, 5700 Magnolia Way
Given by: Shelley Dawson
RSVP: (770) 555-3689

BRIDESMAIDS' LUNCHEON WORKSHEET

Type of Party: _____

Host/Hostess: _____

Phone #: _____

Date: _____

Time: _____

Location: _____

Expected No. of Guests: _____

	Description	Estimated Cost	Actual Cost
Food:			
Beverages:			
Rentals:			
Decorations:			

Total: $_____ $_____

NOTES: _____

_____

_____

_____

GUEST AND GIFT LIST

BRIDESMAIDS' LUNCHEON

Name Telephone No. Street Address City, State, Zip Code	Rsvp How Many ?	Gift	Thank You Sent ✓

*G*UEST AND *G*IFT *L*IST

BRIDESMAIDS' LUNCHEON

Name Telephone No. Street Address City, State, Zip Code	Rsvp How Many ?	Gift	Thank You Sent ✓

GUEST AND GIFT LIST

BRIDESMAIDS' LUNCHEON

Name Telephone No. Street Address City, State, Zip Code	Rsvp How Many ?	Gift	Thank You Sent ✓

$\mathcal{T}$HE BACHELOR PARTY

The bachelor party was originally a simple dinner among the groom and his friends symbolizing his last night out as a single man. It has evolved over the years, and tales of binge drinking and strippers have struck fear in the hearts of brides everywhere. But any groom worthy of marriage should respect his bride and never put himself in a position of dishonoring himself or his future wife.

That having been said, the bachelor party is "boys' night out" and should be a fun and memorable celebration. The best man is usually in charge but the party may be thrown by several of the ushers. It should **not** be thrown the night before the wedding. You and your attendants may need time to recover from the festivities and would not look respectable showing up for the wedding looking tired and run-down.

Many parties start off with dinner and drinks, toasting the groom and his bride-to-be, followed by bar-hopping or attending a gentlemen's club. Make sure you arrange for a designated driver or have enough money for cab fare if drinking will be part of the night. If funds allow, rent a limo or van to take you to your destinations.

If the bar scene is not your thing, try something different like going on a weekend outing with the guys. Camping has always encouraged male bonding. Or go on a sports-related excursion. Exercise your adrenaline by engaging in good old-fashioned competition with your buddies.

Bachelor Party Worksheet

Type of Party: _____

Host/Hostess: _____

Phone #: _____

Date: _____

Time: _____

Location: _____

Expected No. of Guests: _____

	Description	Estimated Cost	Actual Cost
Food:			
Beverages:			
Rentals:			
Decorations:			

Total: $_____ $_____

NOTES: _____
_____
_____
_____

*G*UEST AND *G*IFT *L*IST

BACHELOR PARTY

Name Telephone No. Street Address City, State, Zip Code	Rsvp How Many ?	Gift	Thank You Sent ✓
_____ _____ _____			
_____ _____ _____			
_____ _____ _____			
_____ _____ _____			
_____ _____ _____			
_____ _____ _____			

Guest and Gift List
BACHELOR PARTY

Name Telephone No. Street Address City, State, Zip Code	Rsvp How Many ?	Gift	Thank You Sent ✓
_____ _____ _____ _____			
_____ _____ _____ _____			
_____ _____ _____ _____			
_____ _____ _____ _____			
_____ _____ _____ _____			
_____ _____ _____ _____			

THE BACHELORETTE PARTY

Why should guys have all the fun? In the past, there was no such thing as a bachelorette party. But with equal rights came equal parties! It is perfectly acceptable to throw the bride a party for her last night out as a single woman. The maid of honor can host this party, but if she has already hosted a shower, a bridesmaid or close friend may offer to host instead.

Generally, this party follows the same guidelines as the bachelor party. This celebration marks your last night out as a single woman, and is not an excuse to do something wild you'd regret later. Keep your groom in your mind when celebrating with the girls.

If dinner is how the evening starts off, consider a nice restaurant or the home of the hostess. Some popular places to go are male strip clubs, nightclubs or bars. Again, if you choose to drink, make sure you have a safe ride to and from your destinations. Lots of limo and luxury van companies have package deals just for this sort of occasion.

Alternative ideas for your bachelorette party include going to a spa for the day with your bridesmaids, renting a hotel room and having a slumber party, going to a winery, or having an all-girl party at someone's home, complete with pizza, videos, and fun games. It's up to you. Have fun and enjoy this special time with your closest friends!

Bachelorette Party Worksheet

Type of Party: _____

Host/Hostess: _____

Phone #: _____

Date: _____

Time: _____

Location: _____

Expected No. of Guests: _____

	Description	Estimated Cost	Actual Cost
Food:			
Beverages:			
Rentals:			
Decorations:			

Total: $_____ $ _____

NOTES: _____
_____
_____
_____

Guest and Gift List
BACHELORETTE PARTY

Name Telephone No. Street Address City, State, Zip Code	Rsvp How Many ?	Gift	Thank You Sent ✓

GUEST AND GIFT LIST

BACHELORETTE PARTY

Name Telephone No. Street Address City, State, Zip Code	Rsvp How Many ?	Gift	Thank You Sent ✓

*W*EDDING DAY BREAKFAST/ BRUNCH

If your wedding is in the late afternoon or evening, a brunch or breakfast may be a perfect way to welcome out-of-town guests. A close friend or relative not associated with the wedding may volunteer to host this. Most likely, you will be running around taking care of last minute details but if you do have the time to attend, make sure you and your soon-to-be spouse don't run into each other (if you're superstitious about the bride and groom not seeing each other until they meet at the altar).

As the bride, you may want to have breakfast with your bridesmaids. This is a good way to relax and spend time with your close friends if you haven't had a chance to do so already. (This is especially nice if any of your bridesmaids are from out of town and haven't been able to participate in any other pre-wedding festivities.)

As the groom, this may be an attractive option for you as well. Another suggestion (if it is something that appeals to you and your ushers) is to play a round of golf at a nearby course. It will help to break up the day and ease the tensions that may be mounting as the clock counts down to the "Big Event".

Also see the Rehearsal Dinner section, starting on page 59.

Wedding Day Breakfast Worksheet

Type of Party: _____

Host/Hostess: _____

Phone #: _____

Date: _____

Time: _____

Location: _____

Expected No. of Guests: _____

	Description	Estimated Cost	Actual Cost
Food:			
Beverages:			
Rentals:			
Decorations:			

Total: $_____ $ _____

NOTES: _____

_____

_____

_____

Guest and Gift List
WEDDING DAY BREAKFAST/BRUNCH

Name Telephone No. Street Address City, State, Zip Code	Rsvp How Many ?	Gift	Thank You Sent ✓

GUEST AND GIFT LIST
WEDDING DAY BREAKFAST/BRUNCH

Name Telephone No. Street Address City, State, Zip Code	Rsvp How Many ?	Gift	Thank You Sent ✓

The following are guidelines for addressing invitations for pre-wedding parties and are primarily for formal invitations. Depending on the formality of the occasion, invitations should be sent out ten days to two weeks before the event.

Guidelines For Addressing Invitations

SITUATION	ENVELOPE
Husband and Wife (with same surname)	Mr. and Mrs. Thomas Smith (use middle name, if known)
Husband and Wife (with different surnames)	Ms. Anita Banks Mr. Thomas Smith (wife's name above husband's)
Husband and Wife (wife has professional title)	Dr. Anita Smith Mr. Thomas Smith (wife's name & title above husband's)
Single Woman (regardless of age)	Miss/Ms. Beverly Smith
Single Man	Mr. William Jones
Unmarried Couple Living Together	Mr. Michael Knight Ms. Paula Orlandi
Two Sisters (over 16)	The Misses Mary and Jane Smith (in order of age)
Two Brothers (over 16)	The Messrs. John and Glen Smith (in order of age)
Brothers & Sisters (over 16)	The Misses Smith The Messrs. Smith (name the girls first)
A Brother and Sister (over 16)	Miss Jane Smith and Mr. John Smith (name the girl first)
Widow	Mrs. William Smith
Divorcee	Mrs. Jones Smith (maiden name and former husband's surname)

Personal Notes

THE REHEARSAL

You and your fiancé have probably been to several weddings and even participated in a few, so the ceremony may seem like a simple process, but you are guaranteed to feel more confident and relaxed having practiced a few times. As mentioned in the introduction, a wedding is like a play but this is a one-time performance, so make it look great!

THE LOCATION

The location of the rehearsal will obviously depend on the location of the ceremony. You should consider several things when selecting a location: formality of the ceremony, time of year, the number of guests attending, as well as you and your fiancé's religious affiliations. Some of the more traditional choices for wedding sites include churches, cathedrals, chapels, temples, and synagogues. However, with today's standards often being less traditional, some other options are private homes, gardens, hotels, clubs, halls, parks, museums, yachts, wineries, beaches, and even hot air balloons!

THE TIME

Traditionally, the rehearsal occurs the day before the wedding, but it can be two days before if it conflicts with your religion or you have scheduling difficulties. Some religious sites may have services, and some clubs or hotels may have events taking place the day before, so it is a good idea to confirm your plans with the person in charge of the wedding site before committing to that location.   If your wedding is small or simple, you may feel comfortable without a rehearsal, but most people find it relieves some of the stress and anxiety over what they will be doing, where they will be standing, etc. The time of day is up to you, but generally it is in the late afternoon or early evening, immediately followed by the rehearsal dinner. There will be a lot of running around and last minute details on the rehearsal day, so having the actual rehearsal later in the day usually makes more sense.

THE REHEARSAL ITSELF

The rehearsal is simply a run-through of what will take place at the ceremony. The following is a list of the people who need to attend the rehearsal:

- Bride
- Groom
- Officiant
- Maid of Honor
- Best Man
- Bridesmaids
- Ushers
- Father of the Bride (for Christian ceremony)
- Both sets of parents (for Jewish ceremony)
- Ring Bearer
- Flower Girl
- Vocalists
- Readers
- Musicians
- Any other participants you feel should practice

If you have hired professional musicians or vocalists, they may not feel the need to attend the rehearsal since they perform at weddings on a regular basis. If this makes you uncomfortable, ask them if they would be willing to come to the rehearsal. If this is a big concern, you may want to agree on this before you hire them.

Other family members, spouses or "significant others" who are invited to the rehearsal dinner may be invited to observe the rehearsal. You don't want too many distractions, however, as this is your one shot to make sure the ceremony is exactly the way you want it. This is the time to ask the officiant and/or wedding coordinator any questions or voice any concerns you may have. If you feel uncomfortable with any part of the ceremony, now is the time to speak up and resolve any problems. You will be too busy with details and too excited on your wedding day to think of these things.

Also, make sure every member of the wedding party feels comfortable with his or her part. Do the bridesmaids and ushers know when it is their turn to go? Do the readers/singers, etc. know when to start? Have each participant memorize their cue (a word or phrase said just before to signal that it's their turn). You may also have the officiant look at the appropriate person so he/she knows it's time. If the ceremony is long or complicated, you may want the officiant to announce each song or reading. For example: "And now we will have Ave Maria performed by the bride's sister, Miss Tara Dawson." Or just the title of the piece can be announced.

Attire

The attire for the rehearsal is entirely up to you; however, unless you are having a formal dinner, it is generally kept casual. The bride and groom may dress a little nicer if they wish since they are the unofficial hosts. Collared shirts and khakis for the men and casual dresses or pantsuits for the women are appropriate, depending on the season. The dress can even be more casual if the rehearsal is at a home and/or the atmosphere is very informal. Use your judgment and have your wedding party follow your lead.

The bride usually carries a bouquet of fake flowers during her practice run down the aisle. This bouquet can also be made of bows from gifts she received at pre-wedding parties.

THINGS TO DO ON YOUR REHEARSAL DAY

❑ Review list of things to bring to the rehearsal (see page 54).

❑ Put suitcases in getaway car.

❑ Give your bridesmaids the lipstick, nail polish and accessories you want them to wear for the wedding.

❑ Give best man the officiant's fee and any other checks for service providers. Instruct him to deliver these checks the day of the wedding.

❑ Arrange for someone to bring accessories such as flower basket, ring pillow, guest book & pen, toasting glasses, cake cutting knife and napkins to the ceremony and reception.

❑ Arrange for someone to mail announcements the day after the wedding.

❑ Arrange for someone to return rental items such as tuxedos, slip and cake pillars after the wedding.

❑ Provide each member of your wedding party with a detailed schedule of events for the wedding day.

❑ Review ceremony seating with ushers.

Things to Bring to the Rehearsal

Bride's List:

☐ Wedding announcements (maid of honor to mail after wedding)
☐ Bridesmaids' gifts (if not already given)
☐ Camera and film
☐ Fake bouquet or ribbon bouquet from bridal shower
☐ Groom's gift (if not already given)
☐ Reception maps and wedding programs
☐ Rehearsal information and ceremony formations
☐ Flower girl basket and ring bearer pillow
☐ Seating diagrams for head table and parents' tables
☐ Wedding schedule of events/timeline
☐ Tape player with wedding music

Groom's List:

☐ Bride's gift (if not already given)
☐ Marriage license
☐ Ushers' gifts (if not already given)
☐ Service providers' fees to give to best man or wedding consultant so he/she can pay them at the wedding

WHAT TO PACK FOR THE CEREMONY

If you are too busy with other details, this might be a task to assign to your maid of honor and best man. Simply give them this list:

Bride's List:

- ❑ Aspirin/Alka Seltzer
- ❑ Bobby pins
- ❑ Breath spray/mints
- ❑ Bridal gown
- ❑ Bridal gown box
- ❑ Cake knife
- ❑ Change of clothes for going away
- ❑ Clear nail polish
- ❑ Deodorant
- ❑ Garter
- ❑ Gloves
- ❑ Groom's ring
- ❑ Guest book
- ❑ Hair brush
- ❑ Hair spray
- ❑ Head piece
- ❑ Iron
- ❑ Jewelry
- ❑ Kleenex
- ❑ Lint brush
- ❑ Luggage
- ❑ Make-up
- ❑ Mirror
- ❑ Nail polish
- ❑ Panty hose

- ❑ Passport
- ❑ Perfume
- ❑ Personal camera
- ❑ Plume pen for guest book
- ❑ Powder
- ❑ Purse
- ❑ Safety pins
- ❑ Scotch tape/masking tape
- ❑ Sewing kit
- ❑ Shoes
- ❑ Something old
- ❑ Something new
- ❑ Something borrowed
- ❑ Something blue
- ❑ Spot remover
- ❑ Straight pins
- ❑ Tampons or sanitary napkins
- ❑ Toasting goblets
- ❑ Toothbrush & paste

Groom's List:

- ❑ Airline tickets
- ❑ Announcements
- ❑ Aspirin/Alka Seltzer
- ❑ Breath spray/mints
- ❑ Bride's ring
- ❑ Change of clothes for going away
- ❑ Cologne
- ❑ Cuff Links
- ❑ Cummerbund
- ❑ Deodorant
- ❑ Hair comb
- ❑ Hair spray

- ❏ Kleenex
- ❏ Lint brush
- ❏ Luggage
- ❏ Neck tie
- ❏ Passport
- ❏ Shirt
- ❏ Shoes
- ❏ Socks
- ❏ Toothbrush & paste
- ❏ Tuxedo
- ❏ Underwear

Personal Notes

THE REHEARSAL DINNER

As with the location of the rehearsal, the location of the rehearsal dinner depends on several factors as well: proximity to the rehearsal site, number of guests expected, and formality of the dinner. Popular places to hold rehearsal dinners are: Restaurants, country clubs, banquet rooms, or private homes.

It is customary for the rehearsal dinner to be hosted by the grooms' parents, but this event can also be hosted by other family members, close friends, or a shared expense between the bride and groom's families, especially if there will be a large number of guests or if it is unusually expensive.

The guest list should include: the wedding party, their spouses or dates, both sets of parents, the parents of any children in the ceremony, and any out of town guests. You may also want to include grandparents, aunts, uncles, or any other close relatives or friends if the budget allows. It is also a nice gesture to invite the officiant and his/her spouse.

Generally, the rehearsal dinner is kept informal as this is a time to relax and give thanks to your family, especially your parents, for all the time, money, and effort they have put forth to make your wedding day as special as possible. The dinner is also to honor those family and friends who have traveled near and far to be a part of your special day. This is a good time to visit with these people since you may not be able to do so during the reception. If you choose to have a formal rehearsal dinner, elegant invitations and more formal attire are appropriate.

Formal Invitation:

Mr. and Mrs. Patrick Thomas
invite you to attend the rehearsal dinner
for
Miss Shelley Dawson and Mr. Bryan Thomas
Friday, the nineteenth of March, eight o'clock
Hollowcreek Country Club
Atlanta, Georgia 30350

Regrets Only
(770) 555-4133

Less Formal:

Rehearsal Dinner for
Shelley and Bryan
Friday, March 19th, 8 PM
Hollowcreek Country Club
hosted by
Carolyn and Patrick Thomas
Regrets Only
(770) 555-4133

A cocktail hour is a nice way for the two families to get to know one another and the rest of the wedding party before they sit down for dinner. Be cautious, however, about the amount of alcohol consumed. Drinking too much the night before the wedding is not a good idea. Always designate sober drivers in the event someone does have a little too much to drink, and make sure everyone has a safe ride home.

Dinner should be served immediately after the cocktail hour. The father of the groom, the host, may make the first toast now or wait until after dinner. If toasts are not made before dinner, they should be made right after dinner, and the wedding party should be given their gifts at the same time.

After the dinner, it's a smart idea for the wedding party to get a good night's sleep. You and your spouse-to-be should part at this point, saying your last good-byes as an unmarried couple. This is not a good time for late night partying. No one wants to be tired or sick on this important day, especially one in which a group of people will be watching your every move.

If all the bridesmaids are staying in one place, this may be a good time for them to take care of last minute details, alleviating you of as much stress as possible. The same goes for the ushers. You should try to focus on enjoying your wedding day and reflecting on its importance.

*R*EHEARSAL *D*INNER *W*ORKSHEET

Location: _____

Expected No. of Guests: _____

Contact Person: _____

Phone #: _____

Date: _____

Time: _____

	Description	Estimated Cost	Actual Cost
Food:			
Beverages:			
Rentals:			
Decorations:			

Cost Per Person $_____

Grand Total $_____

NOTES: _____
_____
_____
_____

REHEARSAL DINNER GUEST LIST

Name Street Address City, State, Zip Code	Phone Number	Rsvp How Many?

Rehearsal Dinner Guest List

Name Street Address City, State, Zip Code	Phone Number	Rsvp How Many?

REHEARSAL DINNER GUEST LIST

Name Street Address City, State, Zip Code	Phone Number	Rsvp How Many?

PERSONAL NOTES

Unique Touches

Unless your wedding is very small, you will be so busy taking pictures, making the rounds at each table for brief visits, and generally being the center of attention that you will have very little time for genuine conversation. Making the most of your rehearsal dinner by adding unique touches can really transform a traditional party into an intimate gathering of friends and family.

A PHOTO MONTAGE

A great way to add a personal touch to the dinner is to have a photo montage of you and your fiancé. Have three boards set up at the entrance of the room that will be used for dinner: two boards for pictures of each of you growing up, and one of the two of you, tracing your life together. Guests will get a kick out of seeing how the two of you have changed over the years and what a cute couple you were when you first started dating!

A SLIDE SHOW

What better way to entertain your guests than with a slide show of you and your spouse-to-be! You can collect photos of both of you growing up, as well as pictures of you together throughout your relationship and up until now. You can also include photos of your family and friends, especially wedding party members. You can bring a stereo or CD player and set the whole show to music.

A VIDEO PHOTO MONTAGE

Along those same lines, make a video using childhood pictures and following both of you as you grow up and meet each other. These can be professionally done, completely edited with graphic titles and your favorite music added. Or if you'd like to save money, you can do it yourself with a good stereo and a steady video camera. Simply place your favorite photos on a flat surface and video each picture with the music playing in the background.

PERSONAL PLACECARDS

If you're good at making things by hand, add your own personal touch and make placecards for each of your guests. You can design each one individually or make them all the same. Write their names in calligraphy, use colored pens, draw designs, or apply bows. Find cute little stickers or designs such as wedding bells or a bride and groom to apply to each card. Try to avoid making it look too busy. If you have a lot of out-of-town guests, consider writing each guest's hometown on the card. Your guests will appreciate how much time and care you put into each placecard.

INTRODUCTIONS

If the rehearsal dinner is small enough, you may consider having each guest stand, introduce themselves, tell where he or she is from and their relationship to the bride and groom. This will get everyone acquainted with one another before the wedding as well as encourage conversation between guests who may never have met but have something in common.

*D*ANCING

If you have the space, dancing is always a good icebreaker. It gets everyone up and moving and gives strangers a chance to meet one another. It also gives you, the bride and groom, a chance to practice your moves before you perform your first dance together as husband and wife on your wedding day!

*H*AVE A THEME

If you would like the dinner to be especially relaxed and informal, have a theme party. Have Mexican food, decorate with bright colors, have a piñata, margaritas and it's a fiesta! Going to Hawaii for your honeymoon? Start a little early and break out the leis, pina coladas and Hawaiian shirts and have a luau! The possibilities are endless. Make it upbeat, make it fun, and above all, make it special!

PERSONAL NOTES

MEMORABLE GIFTS

In the months before your wedding, you've probably had a whole team of family and friends working for you, helping you entertain, shop, and plan for the big day. Giving each of them a unique gift is a great way to let them know how much you appreciate all they've done.

Deciding on gifts for members of your wedding party, parents, and any other special people may seem like a difficult task. But with a little creativity, a bit of ingenuity, and a lot of love, your gifts will reflect the sincerity of your gratitude.

THE WEDDING PARTY

MAID OF HONOR: Your maid of honor has probably been the most helpful of all your bridesmaids, helping you shop for your gown, hosting the bridal shower and/or the bachelorette party. You want to get her something nice to reflect your appreciation for her extra efforts. You can go several ways. You can get her the same gift you get the rest of the bridesmaids along with something special just for her, or you can give her a different gift altogether -- one that is extra special.

Traditionally, gifts of jewelry are given as gifts. Especially popular are items that can be engraved with names and dates. But if earrings, bracelets, or picture frames just won't do for your maid of honor, get creative. Treat her to a massage, a day at the spa, or a weekend away with her significant other. If you are childhood friends, find old pictures of the two of you growing up, make a collage and have it framed. Ask people close to her if there's something she's always wanted and would consider special coming from you.

BRIDESMAIDS: Deciding on gifts for your bridesmaids shouldn't be too difficult since you are getting each of them the same thing.   You may want to get them earrings that compliment their bridesmaid gowns.   Try to pick something classic that they can wear after the wedding as well.   Bracelets with their names engraved in them make nice gifts.   Silver picture frames are great gifts not only because you can have their names engraved on them, but also because you can give each bridesmaid a picture of the two of you at the wedding as a memento of the occasion.   If you'd like to do something different, consider making your bridesmaids a gift.   You can put together gift baskets for each bridesmaid with several items that you feel would be meaningful to them.   Or if you're really artistic, make all the items in the basket yourself-- you can make picture frames, candles, ceramics, and jewelry.   Another idea is to buy a book about friendship and highlight individual passages that you feel best describe your friendship with each bridesmaid.   Along those same lines, if you're adept at creative writing, write a poem for each bridesmaid, have it framed, and read each one as you present it!

BEST MAN: Follow the same general guidelines as with the maid of honor. You can get your best man an engraved watch, a nice pen set, or a night or weekend at a bed and breakfast with his significant other. Does he like golf? Get him a nice golf club with his name engraved on it. Find something that reflects his personality or interests. A gift with a lot of thought put into it is always treasured.

USHERS: As mentioned before, engraved gifts are a nice memento with which to remember the wedding and the usher's part in it. Popular gifts for ushers include: engraved pens, money clips, mugs, flasks, or cufflinks. Are your ushers the outdoor types? Consider Swiss-Army knives. Are they golfers? Give each of them a certificate for a round of golf at their favorite course. Again, while the traditional gift is something permanent, it is ultimately left up to you what to give.

OTHER PARTICIPANTS: For other people involved in the wedding, a small token of appreciation is appropriate. Give the reader his/her scripture or passage in an engraved frame. Do the same for the vocalist. If a friend or family member really went out of his or her way to help with the wedding, send flowers, a nice bottle of wine, or a gift certificate for dinner. The flower girl or ring bearer should receive a small gift as well. A picture of you and her/him in a frame is suitable.

PARENTS: Your parents probably deserve a lot of credit and are often forgotten or taken for granted. Give them a nice gift to show your love and appreciation. A picture frame engraved with the wedding date is a great gift as they will surely want a picture of the bride and groom. Or send them on a weekend getaway after the wedding or a romantic dinner for two.

BRIDE'S GIFT: The bride and groom traditionally give each other a gift. This is not mandatory, especially if you've spent a lot on each other's rings and feel those are sufficient as gifts. Be sure, however, to agree in advance whether to give each other gifts to prevent any resentment or embarrassment if only one of you were to get the other something. The groom should get his bride something personal that symbolizes his love for her. This can be a nice piece of jewelry, a framed photo of the two of you, or a charm that she adds to a charm bracelet. A hope chest is a charming gift: it can be filled with wonderful memories of the two of you for years to come.

GROOM'S GIFT: Your gift to the groom should be elegant and meaningful. An engraved watch or pen set are traditional gifts. Another great gift is a beautiful framed photo of you in your wedding gown (you can have this done by your wedding photographer the day of the wedding or at a studio in advance). Also consider gifts you can use on your honeymoon, or perhaps a romantic weekend reserved for sometime in the future after everything has calmed down and you've begun to settle into married life.

UNFORGETTABLE TOASTS

Your rehearsal dinner is a time for family and friends to gather and relax a little before the wedding day, which will inevitably be filled with nervous tension and excitement. This is also a time to thank those who've given of themselves to make your wedding a momentous occasion. Toasting these people is a must! It's also a great way for the wedding party to be introduced to everyone.

ETIQUETTE

Since the majority of the toasts at the wedding reception will be sentimental in nature, the rehearsal dinner toasts should be lighthearted and/or humorous. It's acceptable to lightly poke fun, but make sure not to offend anyone with an off-color remark or embarrass anyone by telling an inappropriate story.

The toasts generally do not take place until everyone has finished eating and champagne (or their beverage of choice) has been poured. This way, the speaker has the audience's full attention. The speaker gets everyone's attention by tapping a spoon on his or her glass. He or she stands, the toast is given and everyone raises their glass to join in toasting the person(s), who is the only one who does not raise his/her glass or take a drink.

If you're the type who doesn't feel comfortable speaking in front of an audience or you do not ad-lib well, you may consider writing your speech down and memorizing it. It shouldn't, however, sound too planned, as if you're reading it off the page. That's a surefire way to lose the audience's attention. A better way may be to write an outline of all the things you'd like to say and have a story or joke to illustrate each point. This way, you can keep on track and avoid babbling.

There is no set time limit for speeches, but nobody likes to hear someone ramble on and on. The shorter the better, especially since it's likely to be an informal setting. If you have a problem wrapping things up, have someone near you signal it's time for you to end your speech.

Above all, make sure you project your voice and don't mumble. Keep your head up and have fun with it!

WHO SHOULD TOAST

Since this is a less formal occasion than the wedding, there are no set rules about who does the toasting. However, if the parents of the groom are hosting the dinner, it is customary that the groom's father make the first toast. He may then turn it over to whoever would like to toast next. If a microphone is being used, it would be logical for the toasts to move from table to table.

This is a perfect opportunity for you, as the bride and groom, to toast your parents for all they've done in the previous months. This may also be a good time to toast those friends and family who've traveled long distances to be there for your wedding day.

If your maid of honor was not planning a toast for the reception, she may want to do so at the rehearsal dinner. The same is true for any family members such as the bride's parents, close family friends, or other honored guests who wish to toast but may not get the chance to do so at the reception.

You may, however, want to put a limit on the toasts to avoid having them go on all night. After a half-hour or so has passed, or you can see the guests are getting restless, the groom's father (or whoever is hosting) should announce that the next toast will be the last.

SAMPLE TOASTS

Here are a few sample toasts with lighthearted, humorous tones that go best with a relaxed, informal atmosphere.

THE GROOM'S FATHER: *I would like to join my wife, Carolyn, in welcoming all of you here tonight and thanking those of you who have traveled distances to be here for Bryan and Shelley's wedding. We hope you enjoyed dinner this evening and look forward to sharing tomorrow's special occasion with all of you.*

Shelley, I'd like to take this time to welcome you into the Thomas family. With three boys, it's about time we added some more grace and beauty to this clan. Shelley, I think I speak for both Bryan's mother and I when I tell you how glad we are that you've come into Bryan's life-- (dramatic pause) to take him out of ours! Just kidding, Bryan.

Actually, Son, we're very impressed with your choice in a bride, and delighted that you summoned up the courage to ask such a beautiful woman to marry you. We remember how shy you once were but I guess those torturous ballroom dancing lessons really paid off! All kidding aside, we couldn't be more pleased that the two of you decided to tie the knot and are very honored to be part of your special day.

Let's all raise our glasses and drink a toast to the bride and groom: Shelley and Bryan.

THE BRIDE AND GROOM (groom starting off): *Thank you, Dad, for that beautifully touching speech. I want to first say that yes, those dance classes did pay off. In fact, I took Shelly dancing on our first date and she's been in a daze ever since, which is probably why she agreed to marry me.*

But seriously, we'd like to thank all of you for being part of this special time. I would particularly like to thank my family since most of you came all the way across the country to be here. It means a lot to me, even though I know my brothers, Sean and Michael, showed up only because they heard weddings were great places to meet single women. So first, let's toast my family and friends, who've traveled near and far to be here this weekend.

I'd also like to thank my ushers, who include my brothers Sean and Michael, along with Tony, my best man, Cameron, and Steve. They've all been such a big help in one way or another, whether it was playing a round of golf to keep me calm or just running errands for me. They're the best friends a guy could ask for and believe me, I've asked for a lot! So here's to my ushers: may they stay conscious during the ceremony and catch me if I don't!

THE BRIDE: *Well, I'd first like to encourage Bryan to stay conscious during the ceremony or he may vow to something he'll regret later!*

Secondly, I would like to reiterate most of what Bryan has already said about family. My family has been absolutely exemplary when it comes to being supportive. My sister Tara has been a wonderful maid of honor, and I couldn't have gotten everything done without her. My little brother, Joe, has been quite a trooper, putting up with all the commotion and hoopla that has surrounded the past few months. And especially my mom and dad, who have so graciously given of their time and money to make this wedding special for Bryan and me and even kept a sense of humor when the bills started rolling in! So I must propose a special toast to my family-- thank you for everything!

And last, but certainly not least, to my bridesmaids- Carrie, Leslie, Amy, and Diane. You guys have done so much over the past months I can't even begin to thank you. Most of all, thank you for taking care of all the little details and hiding any problems from me so I didn't lose my head. And with the exception of the temper tantrum I threw during gown shopping, you've kept me calm, cool, and collected. I know, I know, you'll get revenge during your weddings. But until then, I would like to honor each of you with a toast-- to my bridesmaids, may they still love me even after tomorrow's said and done!

PERSONAL NOTES

Who Pays For What

A breakdown of the traditional wedding expenses

*B*RIDE AND/OR BRIDE'S FAMILY

- Engagement party
- Wedding consultant's fee
- Bridal gown, veil and accessories
- Wedding stationery, calligraphy and postage
- Wedding gift for bridal couple
- Groom's wedding ring
- Gifts for bridesmaids
- Bridesmaids' bouquets
- Pre-wedding parties and bridesmaids' luncheon
- Photography and videography
- Bride's medical exam and blood test
- Wedding guest book and other accessories
- Total cost of the ceremony, including location, flowers, music, rental items and accessories
- Total cost of the reception, including location, flowers, music, rental items, accessories, food, beverages, cake, decorations, favors, etc.
- Transportation for bridal party to ceremony and reception
- Own attire and travel expenses

*G*ROOM AND/OR GROOM'S FAMILY

- Own travel expenses and attire
- Rehearsal dinner
- Wedding gift for bridal couple
- Bride's wedding ring
- Gifts for groom's attendants
- Groom's medical exam and blood test
- Bride's bouquet and going away corsage
- Mothers' and grandmothers' corsages
- All boutonnieres
- Officiant's fee
- Marriage license
- Honeymoon expenses

*A*TTENDANTS

- Own attire except flowers
- Travel expenses
- Bridal shower paid for by maid of honor and bridesmaids
- Bachelor party paid for by best man and ushers

WEDDING PARTY RESPONSIBILITIES

Like a play, each member of your wedding party has his or her own role. In this case, their role is to help your wedding run as smoothly as possible.

The second half of this book contains the *Wedding Party Responsibility Cards*, a convenient way to convey important information to members of your wedding party. Everything they need to know is included on a perforated, pocket-sized card. In addition to itemizing each member's responsibilities, financial and otherwise, these cards also contain useful illustrated formations for the processional, recessional, and altar line-up.

The following is a list of each wedding party member's responsibilities for your own reference.

MAID OF HONOR

The maid of honor is the bride's main consultant and should assist her throughout the planning of the wedding. Her main job should be to relieve the bride of as many duties as possible, especially on the Big Day, so that she may relax and enjoy her wedding celebration. Here is a list of the maid of honor's main responsibilities:

- Helps bride select attire and address invitations.
- Plans bridal shower for bride.
- Arrives at dressing site 2 hours before ceremony to assist bride in dressing.
- Arrives dressed at ceremony site 1 hour before the wedding for photographs.
- Arranges the bride's veil before the processional and the recessional.
- Follows the bridesmaids and precedes ring bearer or flower girl in the processional.
- Stands to the left of the bride and slightly behind her during the ceremony, facing the officiant.
- Holds bride's bouquet and groom's ring, if no ring bearer, during the ceremony.
- Is escorted out by the best man, to his right, immediately following flower girl/ring bearer or bride/groom during the recessional.
- Witnesses the signing of the marriage certificate.
- Stands to the left of the groom in the receiving line.
- Sits to the left of the groom at the head table.
- Keeps the bride on schedule.
- Dances with best man during the bridal party dance.
- Helps the bride change into her going away clothes.

*B*EST MAN

The best man is essentially the groom's right-hand man. He not only offers moral support, but assists the groom with any duties and activities, the main one being the bachelor party. Just like the maid of honor, he should try to relieve the groom of as many duties as possible. Those duties include:

- Responsible for organizing ushers' activities.
- Organizes bachelor party for groom.
- Drives groom to ceremony site and sees that he is properly dressed before the wedding.
- Arrives dressed at ceremony site 1 hour before the wedding for photographs.
- Brings marriage license to wedding.
- Pays the clergyman, musicians, photographer, and any other service providers the day of the wedding.
- Stands to the left of the groom, facing the guests, during the processional.
- Holds the bride's ring for the groom, if no ring bearer, until needed by officiant.
- Escorts maid of honor, to her left, immediately following flower girl/ ring bearer or bride/ groom during the recessional.
- Witnesses the signing of the marriage license.
- Drives newlyweds to reception if no hired driver.
- Offers first toast at reception, usually before dinner.
- Sits to the right of bride at the head table.
- Keeps groom on schedule.
- Dances with maid of honor during the bridal party dance.
- May drive couple to airport or honeymoon suite.
- Oversees return of tuxedo rentals for groom and ushers, on time and in good condition.

Bridesmaids

- Assist maid/matron of honor in planning bridal shower.
- Assist bride with errands and addressing invitations.
- Participate in all pre-wedding parties.
- Arrive at dressing site 2 hours before ceremony.
- Arrive dressed at ceremony site 1 hour before the wedding for photographs.
- Walk behind ushers in order of height during the processional, either in pairs or in single file.
- Stand to the left of maid/matron of honor and slightly behind her during the ceremony, facing the officiant.
- Are escorted out by ushers (to ushers' right) immediately following maid of honor and best man during recessional.
- Stand to the left of the maid of honor in receiving line (optional).
- Sit next to ushers at the head table.
- Dance with ushers and other important guests.
- Encourage single women to participate in the bouquet-tossing ceremony.

Ushers

- Help best man with bachelor party.
- Arrive dressed at ceremony site 1 hour before the wedding for pre-ceremony photographs and to seat guests as they arrive.
- Distribute wedding programs and maps to the reception as guests arrive.
- Seat guests at the ceremony as follows:
    -- If female, offer the right arm.
    -- If male, walk along his left side.

- -- If couple, offer right arm to female; male follows a step or two behind.
- -- Seat bride's guests in left pews.
- -- Seat groom's guests in right pews.
- -- Leave the first several rows of pews open on both sides for seating family members and other VIPs.
- -- Maintain equal number of guests in left and right pews, if possible.
- -- If a group of guests arrive at the same time, seat the eldest woman first.
- -- Just prior to the processional, escort groom's mother to her seat; then escort bride's mother to her seat.
- Two ushers may roll carpet down the aisle after both mothers are seated.
- If pew ribbons are used, two ushers may loosen them one row at a time after the ceremony.
- Direct guests to the reception site.
- Dance with bridesmaids and other important guests.

BRIDE'S MOTHER

- Helps prepare guest list for bride and her family.
- Helps plan the wedding ceremony and reception.
- Helps bride select her bridal gown.
- Helps bride keep track of gifts received.
- Selects her own attire according to the formality and color of the wedding.
- Makes accommodations for bride's out of town guests.
- Arrives dressed at ceremony site 1 hour before the wedding for photographs.
- Is the last person to be seated right before the processional begins.

- Sits in the left front pew to the left of bride's father during the ceremony.
- May stand up to signal the start of the processional.
- Can witness the signing of the marriage license.
- Dances with the groom after the first dance.
- Acts as hostess at the reception.

*B*RIDE'S FATHER

- Helps prepare guest list for bride and her family.
- Selects attire that complements groom's attire.
- Rides to the ceremony with bride in limousine.
- Arrives dressed at ceremony site 1 hour before the wedding for photographs.
- After giving bride away, sits in the left front pew to the right of bride's mother. If divorced, sits in second or third row unless financing the wedding.
- When officiant asks, "Who gives this bride away?" answers, "Her mother and I do" or something similar.
- Can witness the signing of the marriage license.
- Dances with bride after first dance.
- Acts as host at the reception.

GROOM'S MOTHER

- Helps prepare guest list for groom and his family.
- Selects attire that complements mother of the bride's attire.
- Makes accommodations for groom's out-of-town guests.
- With groom's father, plans rehearsal dinner.
- Arrives dressed at ceremony site 1 hour before the wedding for photographs.
- May stand up to signal the start of the processional.
- Can witness the signing of the marriage license.

GROOM'S FATHER

- Helps prepare guest list for groom and his family.
- Selects attire that complements groom's attire.
- With groom's mother, plans rehearsal dinner.
- Offers toast to bride at rehearsal dinner.
- Arrives dressed at ceremony site 1 hour before the wedding for photographs.
- Can witness the signing of the marriage license.

FLOWER GIRL

- Usually between the ages of four and eight.
- Attends rehearsal to practice but is not required to attend pre-wedding parties.
- Arrives dressed at ceremony site 45 minutes before the wedding for photos.
- Carries a basket filled with loose rose petals to strew along bride's path during processional, if allowed by ceremony site.

- If very young, sits with her parents during ceremony.

RING BEARER

- Usually between the ages of four and eight.
- Attends rehearsal to practice but is not required to attend pre-wedding parties.
- Arrives at ceremony site 45 minutes before the wedding for photographs.
- Carries a white pillow with rings attached.
- If younger than 7 years, carries artificial rings.
- If very young, sits with his parents during ceremony. After ceremony, carries ring pillow upside down so artificial rings do not show.

A Final Thought

The months surrounding your wedding are a special time and should be as memorable as possible. It's easy to get caught up in all the plans, details, and stress common to most weddings. If you feel yourself getting entangled in all the commotion, try to remember the real reason for all this fuss: your love and commitment to one another.

May we suggest that at least once during your wedding you stop, take a deep breath, and absorb every detail: every smell, every taste, every touch, feeling, and emotion and savor it for that moment, then tuck it away into your memory for future reflection. Remember, this is a once in a lifetime event!

Personal Notes

PERSONAL NOTES

PERSONAL NOTES

Personal Notes

PERSONAL NOTES

OTHER HELPFUL WEDDING PRODUCTS

Wedding Solutions offers several great products to facilitate the wedding planning process. To order any of these products, simply fill out the Order Form on page 99.

Easy Wedding Planning Plus (EWPP)

A full-sized, complete wedding planner containing numerous worksheets as well as beautiful photographs of popular wedding flowers. A must for planning any wedding!

Easy Wedding Planning (EWP)

A smaller version of *Easy Wedding Planning Plus*. This pocket-sized book offers a full explanation of every aspect of the wedding planning process, organized in a way that is very easy to follow.

The Indispensable Groom's Guide (TIGG)

This handy book offers a full explanation of each aspect of the wedding a groom is typically responsible for: Diamonds, Legal Matters, Formal Wear, Gifts, Bachelor Party, Rehearsal Dinner, Toasts, and much more. A comprehensive honeymoon planner is now also included to assist you in planning the honeymoon of your dreams.

Easy Wedding Planning Software for Windows™ (EWPS)

This wedding planning software is extremely easy to use and allows you to keep track of your guest list, gifts received, and service providers; perform a detailed budget analysis; maintain a checklist of things to do; and much more. This professional software is available through Wedding Solutions for $34.95. As a special offer to our readers, you may order it for only $19.95.

Easy Wedding Planning Checklist (EWPC)

A large and convenient poster (9.5" x 23") which shows, at a glance, a chronological list of everything you must do when planning your wedding. This checklist is available through Wedding Solutions for $5.95. As a special offer to our readers, you may order it **FREE OF CHARGE**. Simply send $2.95 for shipping and handling.

After The Wedding (ATW)

This book of attractive, colorful labels will convert 25 of your favorite wedding and honeymoon photographs into unique and memorable postcards. Use these postcards to send short notes or a memento of your most special day to friends and family.

Naughty Games for the Honeymoon... and Beyond (NGH)

This unique book is a must-have for every newlywed! Featuring 50 sealed "naughty" games guaranteed to make every moment of your honeymoon memorable. Get a little adventurous while bringing a deeper level of intimacy and passion to your new marriage!

ORDER FORM

The following abbreviations are explained on pages 97-98.

	QTY.		COST		TOTAL
(EWPP)	_____	x	$19.95	=	$ _____
(EWP)	_____	x	$ 6.95	=	$ _____
(TIGG)	_____	x	$ 6.95	=	$ _____
(WPRC)	_____	x	$ 6.95	=	$ _____
(EWPS)	_____	x	$19.95	=	$ _____
(EWPC)	_____	x	~~$ 5.95~~	=	$ FREE
(ATW)	_____	x	$ 8.95	=	$ _____
(NGH)	_____	x	$17.95	=	$ _____

Subtotal: $ _____

**California Residents
add 7.75% tax:** $ _____

Shipping And Handling: $ _____
(add $2.95 for first item ordered
and $1.00 for each additional item)

Grand Total: $ _____

**Please fill out the back of this form, cut along the dotted line and
mail to Wedding Solutions along with your check or money
order.**

Cut along dotted line and send to Wedding Solutions
at 6347 Caminito Tenedor, San Diego, CA 92120,
along with check or money order.

WEDDING SOLUTIONS
6347 Caminito Tenedor
San Diego, CA 92120

Name: _____

Street: _____

City/State/Zip: _____

WEDDING PARTY RESPONSIBILITY CARDS

The following cards will provide your wedding party with everything they need to know to assure a picture perfect wedding.

Tear out these cards and give one to each member of your wedding party. With these cards, they will learn what to do, how to do it, when to arrive, and what their positions are during the Processional, Ceremony, and Recessional.

Christian Ceremony = Blue Heading Cards

Jewish Ceremony = Green Heading Cards

MAID OF HONOR

- Helps bride select attire and address invitations.
- Plans bridal shower for bride.
- Arrives at dressing site 2 hours before ceremony to assist bride in dressing.
- Arrives dressed at ceremony site 1 hour before the wedding for photographs.
- Arranges the bride's veil and train before the processional and recessional.
- Follows bridesmaids and precedes ring bearer or flower girl in the processional.
- Stands to the left of bride and slightly behind her during the ceremony, facing the officiant.
- Holds bride's bouquet and groom's ring, if no ring bearer, during the ceremony.
- Is escorted out by best man, to his right, immediately following flower girl/ring bearer or bride/groom during the recessional.
- Witnesses the signing of the marriage certificate.
- Stands to the left of groom in the receiving line.
- Sits to the left of groom at the head table.
- Keeps bride on schedule.
- Dances with best man during the bridal party dance.
- Helps bride change into her going away clothes.

FINANCIAL RESPONSIBILITIES TYPICALLY INCLUDE:

- Own attire except flowers
- Travel expenses

BEST MAN

- Responsible for organizing ushers' activities.
- Organizes bachelor party for groom.
- Drives groom to ceremony site and sees that he is properly dressed before the wedding.
- Arrives dressed at ceremony site 1 hour before the wedding for photographs.
- Brings marriage license to wedding.
- Pays the clergyman, musicians, and any other service providers the day of the wedding.
- Stands to the left of the groom, facing the guests, during the processional.
- Stands to the right of groom and slightly behind him during the ceremony, facing the officiant.
- Holds the bride's ring for the groom, if no ring bearer, until needed by officiant.
- Escorts maid of honor, to her left, immediately following flower girl/ring bearer or bride/groom during the recessional.
- Witnesses the signing of the marriage certificate.
- Drives newlyweds to reception if no hired driver.
- Offers first toast at reception, usually before dinner.
- Sits to the right of bride at the head table.
- Keeps groom on schedule.
- Dances with maid of honor during the bridal party dance.
- May drive couple to airport or honeymoon suite.
- Oversees return of tuxedo rentals for groom and ushers, on time and in good condition.

FINANCIAL RESPONSIBILITIES TYPICALLY INCLUDE:

- Own attire except boutonniere
- Travel expenses

CHRISTIAN CEREMONY FORMATIONS

Processional

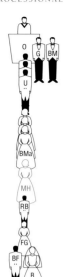

Recessional

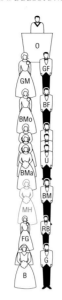

Altar Line Up

Bride's Pews   Groom's Pews

ABBREVIATIONS

B = Bride
G = Groom
BM = Best Man
MH = Maid of Honor
BF = Bride's Father
BMo = Bride's Mother

GF = Groom's Father
GM = Groom's Mother
BMa = Bridesmaids
U = Ushers
FG = Flower Girl
RB = Ring Bearer
O = Officiant

CHRISTIAN CEREMONY FORMATIONS

Processional

Recessional

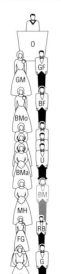

Altar Line Up

Bride's Pews   Groom's Pews

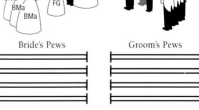

ABBREVIATIONS

B = Bride
G = Groom
BM = Best Man
MH = Maid of Honor
BF = Bride's Father
BMo = Bride's Mother

GF = Groom's Father
GM = Groom's Mother
BMa = Bridesmaids
U = Ushers
FG = Flower Girl
RB = Ring Bearer
O = Officiant

TRADITIONAL RESPONSIBILITIES

ℬRIDESMAIDS

- Assist maid/matron of honor in planning bridal shower.

- Assist bride with errands and addressing invitations.

- Participate in all pre-wedding parties.

- Arrive at dressing site 2 hours before ceremony.

- Arrive dressed at ceremony site 1 hour before the wedding for photographs.

- Walk behind ushers in order of height during the processional, either in pairs or in single file.

- Stand to the left of maid/matron of honor and slightly behind her during the ceremony, facing the officiant.

- Are escorted out by ushers (to ushers' right) immediately following maid of honor and best man during recessional.

- Stand to left of maid of honor in receiving line (optional).

- Sit next to ushers at the head table.

- Dance with ushers and other important guests.

- Encourage single women to participate in the bouquet-tossing ceremony.

FINANCIAL RESPONSIBILITIES TYPICALLY INCLUDE:

- Own attire except flowers

- Travel expenses

TRADITIONAL RESPONSIBILITIES

ℬRIDESMAIDS

- Assist maid/matron of honor in planning bridal shower.

- Assist bride with errands and addressing invitations.

- Participate in all pre-wedding parties.

- Arrive at dressing site 2 hours before ceremony.

- Arrive dressed at ceremony site 1 hour before the wedding for photographs.

- Walk behind ushers in order of height during the processional, either in pairs or in single file.

- Stand to the left of maid/matron of honor and slightly behind her during the ceremony, facing the officiant.

- Are escorted out by ushers (to ushers' right) immediately following maid of honor and best man during recessional.

- Stand to left of maid of honor in receiving line (optional).

- Sit next to ushers at the head table.

- Dance with ushers and other important guests.

- Encourage single women to participate in the bouquet-tossing ceremony.

FINANCIAL RESPONSIBILITIES TYPICALLY INCLUDE:

- Own attire except flowers

- Travel expenses

CHRISTIAN CEREMONY FORMATIONS

*P*ROCESSIONAL   *R*ECESSIONAL   *A*LTAR *L*INE *U*P

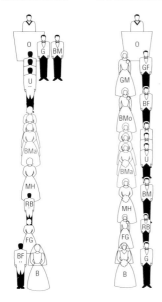

Bride's Pews   Groom's Pews

ABBREVIATIONS

B = Bride	GF = Groom's Father
G = Groom	GM = Groom's Mother
BM = Best Man	BMa = Bridesmaids
MH = Maid of Honor	U = Ushers
BF = Bride's Father	FG = Flower Girl
BMo = Bride's Mother	RB = Ring Bearer
	O = Officiant

CHRISTIAN CEREMONY FORMATIONS

*P*ROCESSIONAL   *R*ECESSIONAL   *A*LTAR *L*INE *U*P

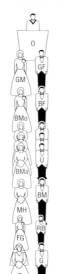

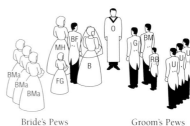

Bride's Pews   Groom's Pews

ABBREVIATIONS

B = Bride	GF = Groom's Father
G = Groom	GM = Groom's Mother
BM = Best Man	BMa = Bridesmaids
MH = Maid of Honor	U = Ushers
BF = Bride's Father	FG = Flower Girl
BMo = Bride's Mother	RB = Ring Bearer
	O = Officiant

ℬRIDESMAIDS

- Assist maid/matron of honor in planning bridal shower.
- Assist bride with errands and addressing invitations.
- Participate in all pre-wedding parties.
- Arrive at dressing site 2 hours before ceremony.
- Arrive dressed at ceremony site 1 hour before the wedding for photographs.
- Walk behind ushers in order of height during the processional, either in pairs or in single file.
- Stand to the left of maid/matron of honor and slightly behind her during the ceremony, facing the officiant.
- Are escorted out by ushers (to ushers' right) immediately following maid of honor and best man during recessional.
- Stand to left of maid of honor in receiving line (optional).
- Sit next to ushers at the head table.
- Dance with ushers and other important guests.
- Encourage single women to participate in the bouquet-tossing ceremony.

FINANCIAL RESPONSIBILITIES TYPICALLY INCLUDE:

- Own attire except flowers
- Travel expenses

TRADITIONAL RESPONSIBILITIES

ℬRIDESMAIDS

- Assist maid/matron of honor in planning bridal shower.
- Assist bride with errands and addressing invitations.
- Participate in all pre-wedding parties.
- Arrive at dressing site 2 hours before ceremony.
- Arrive dressed at ceremony site 1 hour before the wedding for photographs.
- Walk behind ushers in order of height during the processional, either in pairs or in single file.
- Stand to the left of maid/matron of honor and slightly behind her during the ceremony, facing the officiant.
- Are escorted out by ushers (to ushers' right) immediately following maid of honor and best man during recessional.
- Stand to left of maid of honor in receiving line (optional).
- Sit next to ushers at the head table.
- Dance with ushers and other important guests.
- Encourage single women to participate in the bouquet-tossing ceremony.

FINANCIAL RESPONSIBILITIES TYPICALLY INCLUDE:

- Own attire except flowers
- Travel expenses

CHRISTIAN CEREMONY FORMATIONS

Processional

Recessional

Altar Line Up

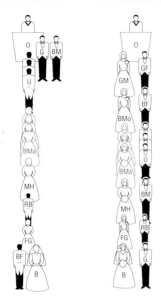

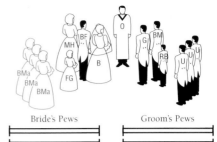

Bride's Pews   Groom's Pews

ABBREVIATIONS

B = Bride	GF = Groom's Father
G = Groom	GM = Groom's Mother
BM = Best Man	BMa = Bridesmaids
MH = Maid of Honor	U = Ushers
BF = Bride's Father	FG = Flower Girl
BMo = Bride's Mother	RB = Ring Bearer
	O = Officiant

CHRISTIAN CEREMONY FORMATIONS

Processional

Recessional

Altar Line Up

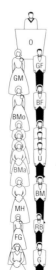

Bride's Pews   Groom's Pews

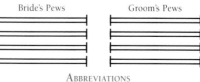

ABBREVIATIONS

B = Bride	GF = Groom's Father
G = Groom	GM = Groom's Mother
BM = Best Man	BMa = Bridesmaids
MH = Maid of Honor	U = Ushers
BF = Bride's Father	FG = Flower Girl
BMo = Bride's Mother	RB = Ring Bearer
	O = Officiant

$\mathscr{B}$RIDESMAIDS

- Assist maid/matron of honor in planning bridal shower.
- Assist bride with errands and addressing invitations.
- Participate in all pre-wedding parties.
- Arrive at dressing site 2 hours before ceremony.
- Arrive dressed at ceremony site 1 hour before the wedding for photographs.
- Walk behind ushers in order of height during the processional, either in pairs or in single file.
- Stand to the left of maid/matron of honor and slightly behind her during the ceremony, facing the officiant.

- Are escorted out by ushers (to ushers' right) immediately following maid of honor and best man during recessional.
- Stand to left of maid of honor in receiving line (optional).
- Sit next to ushers at the head table.
- Dance with ushers and other important guests.
- Encourage single women to participate in the bouquet-tossing ceremony.

FINANCIAL RESPONSIBILITIES TYPICALLY INCLUDE:

- Own attire except flowers
- Travel expenses

TRADITIONAL RESPONSIBILITIES

$\mathscr{B}$RIDESMAIDS

- Assist maid/matron of honor in planning bridal shower.
- Assist bride with errands and addressing invitations.
- Participate in all pre-wedding parties.
- Arrive at dressing site 2 hours before ceremony.
- Arrive dressed at ceremony site 1 hour before the wedding for photographs.
- Walk behind ushers in order of height during the processional, either in pairs or in single file.
- Stand to the left of maid/matron of honor and slightly behind her during the ceremony, facing the officiant.

- Are escorted out by ushers (to ushers' right) immediately following maid of honor and best man during recessional.
- Stand to left of maid of honor in receiving line (optional).
- Sit next to ushers at the head table.
- Dance with ushers and other important guests.
- Encourage single women to participate in the bouquet-tossing ceremony.

FINANCIAL RESPONSIBILITIES TYPICALLY INCLUDE:

- Own attire except flowers
- Travel expenses

𝒫ROCESSIONAL   ℛECESSIONAL   𝒜LTAR ℒINE 𝒰P

Bride's Pews   Groom's Pews

ABBREVIATIONS

B = Bride	GF = Groom's Father
G = Groom	GM = Groom's Mother
BM = Best Man	BMa = Bridesmaids
MH = Maid of Honor	U = Ushers
BF = Bride's Father	FG = Flower Girl
BMo = Bride's Mother	RB = Ring Bearer
	O = Officiant

CHRISTIAN CEREMONY FORMATIONS

𝒫ROCESSIONAL   ℛECESSIONAL   𝒜LTAR ℒINE 𝒰P

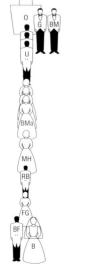

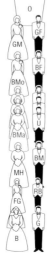

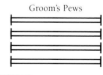

Bride's Pews   Groom's Pews

ABBREVIATIONS

B = Bride	GF = Groom's Father
G = Groom	GM = Groom's Mother
BM = Best Man	BMa = Bridesmaids
MH = Maid of Honor	U = Ushers
BF = Bride's Father	FG = Flower Girl
BMo = Bride's Mother	RB = Ring Bearer
	O = Officiant

TRADITIONAL RESPONSIBILITIES

𝒰SHERS

- Help best man with bachelor party.
- Arrive dressed at ceremony site 1 hour before the wedding for pre-ceremony photographs and to seat guests as they arrive.
- Distribute wedding programs and maps to the reception as guests arrive.
- Seat guests at the ceremony as follows:
  - If female, offer the right arm.
  - If male, walk along his left side.
  - If couple, offer right arm to female; male follows a step or two behind.
  - Seat bride's guests in left pews.
  - Seat groom's guests in right pews.
  - Leave the first several rows of pews open on both sides for seating family members and other VIPs.
  - Maintain equal number of guests in left and right pews, if possible.
  - Should a group of guests arrive at the same time, seat the eldest woman first.
  - Just prior to the processional, escort groom's mother to her seat; then escort bride's mother to her seat.

- Two ushers may roll carpet down the aisle after both mothers are seated.
- Lead the procession in order of height, either in pairs or in single file.
- Stand to the right of best man and slightly behind him during ceremony, facing the officiant.
- Escort bridesmaids (to bridesmaids' left) immediately following maid of honor and best man during recessional.
- If pew ribbons are used, two ushers may loosen them one row at a time after the ceremony.
- Keep an eye out for items left in pews.
- Direct guests to the reception site.
- Sit at the head table next to bridesmaids.
- Dance with bridesmaids and other important guests.
- Encourage single men to participate in the garter ceremony.

FINANCIAL RESPONSIBILITIES TYPICALLY INCLUDE:
- Own attire except boutonniere
- Travel expenses

TRADITIONAL RESPONSIBILITIES

𝒰SHERS

- Help best man with bachelor party.
- Arrive dressed at ceremony site 1 hour before the wedding for pre-ceremony photographs and to seat guests as they arrive.
- Distribute wedding programs and maps to the reception as guests arrive.
- Seat guests at the ceremony as follows:
  - If female, offer the right arm.
  - If male, walk along his left side.
  - If couple, offer right arm to female; male follows a step or two behind.
  - Seat bride's guests in left pews.
  - Seat groom's guests in right pews.
  - Leave the first several rows of pews open on both sides for seating family members and other VIPs.
  - Maintain equal number of guests in left and right pews, if possible.
  - Should a group of guests arrive at the same time, seat the eldest woman first.
  - Just prior to the processional, escort groom's mother to her seat; then escort bride's mother to her seat.

- Two ushers may roll carpet down the aisle after both mothers are seated.
- Lead the procession in order of height, either in pairs or in single file.
- Stand to the right of best man and slightly behind him during ceremony, facing the officiant.
- Escort bridesmaids (to bridesmaids' left) immediately following maid of honor and best man during recessional.
- If pew ribbons are used, two ushers may loosen them one row at a time after the ceremony.
- Keep an eye out for items left in pews.
- Direct guests to the reception site.
- Sit at the head table next to bridesmaids.
- Dance with bridesmaids and other important guests.
- Encourage single men to participate in the garter ceremony.

FINANCIAL RESPONSIBILITIES TYPICALLY INCLUDE:
- Own attire except boutonniere
- Travel expenses

CHRISTIAN CEREMONY FORMATIONS

Processional *Recessional* *Altar Line Up*

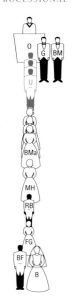

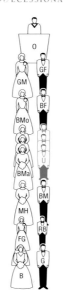

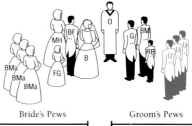

Bride's Pews   Groom's Pews

ABBREVIATIONS

B = Bride
G = Groom
BM = Best Man
MH = Maid of Honor
BF = Bride's Father
BMo = Bride's Mother

GF = Groom's Father
GM = Groom's Mother
BMa = Bridesmaids
U = Ushers
FG = Flower Girl
RB = Ring Bearer
O = Officiant

CHRISTIAN CEREMONY FORMATIONS

Processional *Recessional* *Altar Line Up*

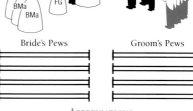

Bride's Pews   Groom's Pews

ABBREVIATIONS

B = Bride
G = Groom
BM = Best Man
MH = Maid of Honor
BF = Bride's Father
BMo = Bride's Mother

GF = Groom's Father
GM = Groom's Mother
BMa = Bridesmaids
U = Ushers
FG = Flower Girl
RB = Ring Bearer
O = Officiant

TRADITIONAL RESPONSIBILITIES

*U*SHERS

- Help best man with bachelor party.
- Arrive dressed at ceremony site 1 hour before the wedding for pre-ceremony photographs and to seat guests as they arrive.
- Distribute wedding programs and maps to the reception as guests arrive.
- Seat guests at the ceremony as follows:
  - If female, offer the right arm.
  - If male, walk along his left side.
  - If couple, offer right arm to female; male follows a step or two behind.
  - Seat bride's guests in left pews.
  - Seat groom's guests in right pews.
  - Leave the first several rows of pews open on both sides for seating family members and other VIPs.
  - Maintain equal number of guests in left and right pews, if possible.
  - Should a group of guests arrive at the same time, seat the eldest woman first.
  - Just prior to the processional, escort groom's mother to her seat; then escort bride's mother to her seat.

- Two ushers may roll carpet down the aisle after both mothers are seated.
- Lead the procession in order of height, either in pairs or in single file.
- Stand to the right of best man and slightly behind him during ceremony, facing the officiant.
- Escort bridesmaids (to bridesmaids' left) immediately following maid of honor and best man during recessional.
- If pew ribbons are used, two ushers may loosen them one row at a time after the ceremony.
- Keep an eye out for items left in pews.
- Direct guests to the reception site.
- Sit at the head table next to bridesmaids.
- Dance with bridesmaids and other important guests.
- Encourage single men to participate in the garter ceremony.

FINANCIAL RESPONSIBILITIES TYPICALLY INCLUDE:
- Own attire except boutonniere
- Travel expenses

TRADITIONAL RESPONSIBILITIES

*U*SHERS

- Help best man with bachelor party.
- Arrive dressed at ceremony site 1 hour before the wedding for pre-ceremony photographs and to seat guests as they arrive.
- Distribute wedding programs and maps to the reception as guests arrive.
- Seat guests at the ceremony as follows:
  - If female, offer the right arm.
  - If male, walk along his left side.
  - If couple, offer right arm to female; male follows a step or two behind.
  - Seat bride's guests in left pews.
  - Seat groom's guests in right pews.
  - Leave the first several rows of pews open on both sides for seating family members and other VIPs.
  - Maintain equal number of guests in left and right pews, if possible.
  - Should a group of guests arrive at the same time, seat the eldest woman first.
  - Just prior to the processional, escort groom's mother to her seat; then escort bride's mother to her seat.

- Two ushers may roll carpet down the aisle after both mothers are seated.
- Lead the procession in order of height, either in pairs or in single file.
- Stand to the right of best man and slightly behind him during ceremony, facing the officiant.
- Escort bridesmaids (to bridesmaids' left) immediately following maid of honor and best man during recessional.
- If pew ribbons are used, two ushers may loosen them one row at a time after the ceremony.
- Keep an eye out for items left in pews.
- Direct guests to the reception site.
- Sit at the head table next to bridesmaids.
- Dance with bridesmaids and other important guests.
- Encourage single men to participate in the garter ceremony.

FINANCIAL RESPONSIBILITIES TYPICALLY INCLUDE:
- Own attire except boutonniere
- Travel expenses

CHRISTIAN CEREMONY FORMATIONS

PROCESSIONAL *RECESSIONAL* *ALTAR LINE UP*

Bride's Pews   Groom's Pews

ABBREVIATIONS

B = Bride	GF = Groom's Father
G = Groom	GM = Groom's Mother
BM = Best Man	BMa = Bridesmaids
MH = Maid of Honor	U = Ushers
BF = Bride's Father	FG = Flower Girl
BMo = Bride's Mother	RB = Ring Bearer
	O = Officiant

CHRISTIAN CEREMONY FORMATIONS

PROCESSIONAL *RECESSIONAL* *ALTAR LINE UP*

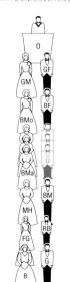

Bride's Pews   Groom's Pews

ABBREVIATIONS

B = Bride	GF = Groom's Father
G = Groom	GM = Groom's Mother
BM = Best Man	BMa = Bridesmaids
MH = Maid of Honor	U = Ushers
BF = Bride's Father	FG = Flower Girl
BMo = Bride's Mother	RB = Ring Bearer
	O = Officiant

TRADITIONAL RESPONSIBILITIES

𝒰SHERS

- Help best man with bachelor party.
- Arrive dressed at ceremony site 1 hour before the wedding for pre-ceremony photographs and to seat guests as they arrive.
- Distribute wedding programs and maps to the reception as guests arrive.
- Seat guests at the ceremony as follows:
  - If female, offer the right arm.
  - If male, walk along his left side.
  - If couple, offer right arm to female; male follows a step or two behind.
  - Seat bride's guests in left pews.
  - Seat groom's guests in right pews.
  - Leave the first several rows of pews open on both sides for seating family members and other VIPs.
  - Maintain equal number of guests in left and right pews, if possible.
  - Should a group of guests arrive at the same time, seat the eldest woman first.
  - Just prior to the processional, escort groom's mother to her seat; then escort bride's mother to her seat.
- Two ushers may roll carpet down the aisle after both mothers are seated.
- Lead the procession in order of height, either in pairs or in single file.
- Stand to the right of best man and slightly behind him during ceremony, facing the officiant.
- Escort bridesmaids (to bridesmaids' left) immediately following maid of honor and best man during recessional.
- If pew ribbons are used, two ushers may loosen them one row at a time after the ceremony.
- Keep an eye out for items left in pews.
- Direct guests to the reception site.
- Sit at the head table next to bridesmaids.
- Dance with bridesmaids and other important guests.
- Encourage single men to participate in the garter ceremony.

FINANCIAL RESPONSIBILITIES TYPICALLY INCLUDE:
- Own attire except boutonniere
- Travel expenses

TRADITIONAL RESPONSIBILITIES

𝒰SHERS

- Help best man with bachelor party.
- Arrive dressed at ceremony site 1 hour before the wedding for pre-ceremony photographs and to seat guests as they arrive.
- Distribute wedding programs and maps to the reception as guests arrive.
- Seat guests at the ceremony as follows:
  - If female, offer the right arm.
  - If male, walk along his left side.
  - If couple, offer right arm to female; male follows a step or two behind.
  - Seat bride's guests in left pews.
  - Seat groom's guests in right pews.
  - Leave the first several rows of pews open on both sides for seating family members and other VIPs.
  - Maintain equal number of guests in left and right pews, if possible.
  - Should a group of guests arrive at the same time, seat the eldest woman first.
  - Just prior to the processional, escort groom's mother to her seat; then escort bride's mother to her seat.
- Two ushers may roll carpet down the aisle after both mothers are seated.
- Lead the procession in order of height, either in pairs or in single file.
- Stand to the right of best man and slightly behind him during ceremony, facing the officiant.
- Escort bridesmaids (to bridesmaids' left) immediately following maid of honor and best man during recessional.
- If pew ribbons are used, two ushers may loosen them one row at a time after the ceremony.
- Keep an eye out for items left in pews.
- Direct guests to the reception site.
- Sit at the head table next to bridesmaids.
- Dance with bridesmaids and other important guests.
- Encourage single men to participate in the garter ceremony.

FINANCIAL RESPONSIBILITIES TYPICALLY INCLUDE:
- Own attire except boutonniere
- Travel expenses

PROCESSIONAL   RECESSIONAL   ALTAR LINE UP

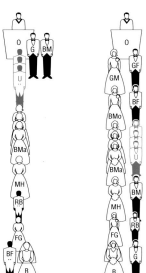

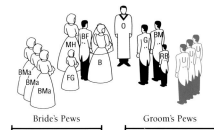

Bride's Pews   Groom's Pews

ABBREVIATIONS

B = Bride	GF = Groom's Father
G = Groom	GM = Groom's Mother
BM = Best Man	BMa = Bridesmaids
MH = Maid of Honor	U = Ushers
BF = Bride's Father	FG = Flower Girl
BMo = Bride's Mother	RB = Ring Bearer
	O = Officiant

PROCESSIONAL   RECESSIONAL   ALTAR LINE UP

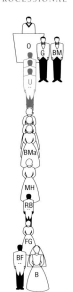

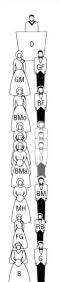

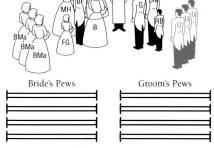

Bride's Pews   Groom's Pews

ABBREVIATIONS

B = Bride	GF = Groom's Father
G = Groom	GM = Groom's Mother
BM = Best Man	BMa = Bridesmaids
MH = Maid of Honor	U = Ushers
BF = Bride's Father	FG = Flower Girl
BMo = Bride's Mother	RB = Ring Bearer
	O = Officiant

TRADITIONAL RESPONSIBILITIES

MOTHER OF THE BRIDE

- Helps prepare guest list for bride and her family.
- Helps plan the wedding ceremony and reception.
- Helps bride select her bridal gown.
- Helps bride keep track of gifts received.
- Selects her own attire according to the formality and color of the wedding.
- Makes accommodations for bride's out of town guests.
- Arrives dressed at ceremony site 1 hour before the wedding for photographs.
- Is escorted down the aisle by best man or head usher, to his right, before the processional begins.
- Is the last person to be seated right before the processional begins.
- Sits in the left front pew to the left of bride's father during the ceremony.
- Stands up to signal the start of the processional.
- Is escorted out by bride's father, to his right, immediately following last bridesmaid and usher during recessional.
- Can witness the signing of the marriage certificate.
- Stands at the head of the receiving line.
- Sits to the right of bride's father at parents' table during reception.

- Dances with the groom after the first dance.
- Acts as hostess at the reception.

ALONG WITH BRIDE'S FATHER AND/OR BRIDE, FINANCIAL RESPONSIBILITIES TYPICALLY INCLUDE:

- Engagement party
- Wedding consultant's fee
- Bridal gown, veil and accessories
- Wedding stationery, calligraphy and postage
- Wedding gift for bridal couple
- Groom's wedding ring
- Gifts for bridesmaids
- Pre-wedding parties and bridesmaids' luncheon
- Photography and videography
- Bride's medical exam and blood test
- Wedding guest book and other accessories
- Rental fee for ceremony site including flowers, music and accessories
- Total cost of reception including rental fees, food, beverages, music, cake, flowers, decorations, favors, etc.
- Transportation for bridal party to ceremony and reception
- Own attire and travel expenses

TRADITIONAL RESPONSIBILITIES

FATHER OF THE BRIDE

- Helps prepare guest list for bride and her family.
- Selects attire that complements groom's attire.
- Rides to the ceremony with bride in limousine.
- Arrives dressed at ceremony site 1 hour before the wedding for photographs.
- Escorts bride down the aisle, to her left, during processional. (In Catholic ceremonies, father of bride may be to the bride's right).
- After giving bride away, sits in the left front pew to the right of bride's mother. If divorced, sits in second or third row unless financing the wedding.
- When officiant asks, "Who gives this bride away?" answers, "Her mother and I do" or something similar.
- Escorts bride's mother, to her left, immediately following last bridesmaid and usher during the recessional.
- Can witness the signing of the marriage certificate.
- Stands to the left of bride's mother in the receiving line (optional).
- Sits to the left of bride's mother at parents' table during reception.
- Dances with bride after first dance.
- Acts as host at the reception.

ALONG WITH BRIDE'S MOTHER AND/OR BRIDE, FINANCIAL RESPONSIBILITIES TYPICALLY INCLUDE:

- Engagement party
- Wedding consultant's fee
- Bridal gown, veil and accessories
- Wedding stationery, calligraphy and postage
- Wedding gift for bridal couple
- Groom's wedding ring
- Gifts for bridesmaids
- Pre-wedding parties and bridesmaids' luncheon
- Photography and videography
- Bride's medical exam and blood test
- Wedding guest book and other accessories
- Rental fee for ceremony site including flowers, music and accessories
- Total cost of reception including rental fees, food, beverages, music, cake, flowers, decorations, favors, etc.
- Transportation for bridal party to ceremony and reception
- Own attire and travel expenses

CHRISTIAN CEREMONY FORMATIONS

PROCESSIONAL

RECESSIONAL

ALTAR LINE UP

Bride's Pews

Groom's Pews

ABBREVIATIONS

B = Bride
G = Groom
BM = Best Man
MH = Maid of Honor
BF = Bride's Father
BMo = Bride's Mother

GF = Groom's Father
GM = Groom's Mother
BMa = Bridesmaids
U = Ushers
FG = Flower Girl
RB = Ring Bearer
O = Officiant

CHRISTIAN CEREMONY FORMATIONS

PROCESSIONAL

RECESSIONAL

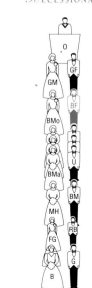

ALTAR LINE UP

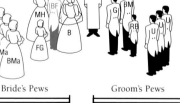

Bride's Pews

Groom's Pews

ABBREVIATIONS

B = Bride
G = Groom
BM = Best Man
MH = Maid of Honor
BF = Bride's Father
BMo = Bride's Mother

GF = Groom's Father
GM = Groom's Mother
BMa = Bridesmaids
U = Ushers
FG = Flower Girl
RB = Ring Bearer
O = Officiant

MOTHER OF THE GROOM

- Helps prepare guest list for groom and his family.
- Selects attire that complements mother of the bride's attire.
- Makes accommodations for groom's out of town guests.
- With groom's father, plans rehearsal dinner.
- Arrives dressed at ceremony site 1 hour before the wedding for photographs.
- Is escorted down the aisle by best man or head usher, to his right, before mother of the bride is seated.
- Sits in the right front pew to the right of groom's father during the ceremony.
- Is escorted out by groom's father, to his right, immediately following bride's parents during the recessional.
- Can witness the signing of the marriage certificate.
- Stands to the left of bride's parents in the receiving line.
- Sits to the right of groom's father at parents' table during reception.

ALONG WITH GROOM'S FATHER AND/OR GROOM, FINANCIAL RESPONSIBILITIES TYPICALLY INCLUDE:

- Own travel expenses and attire
- Rehearsal dinner
- Wedding gift for bridal couple
- Bride's wedding ring
- Gifts for groom's attendants
- Medical exam for groom including blood test
- Bride's bouquet and going away corsage
- Mothers' and grandmothers' corsages
- All boutonnieres
- Officiant's fee
- Marriage license
- Honeymoon expenses

FATHER OF THE GROOM

- Helps prepare guest list for groom and his family.
- Selects attire that complements groom's attire.
- With groom's mother, plans rehearsal dinner.
- Offers toast to bride at rehearsal dinner.
- Arrives dressed at ceremony site 1 hour before the wedding for photographs.
- Follows mother of the groom as she is escorted by best man or head usher before the processional begins.
- Sits in the right front pew to the left of groom's mother during the ceremony.
- Escorts groom's mother, to her left, immediately following bride's parents during the recessional.
- Can witness the signing of the marriage certificate.
- Stands to the left of the groom's mother and to the right of the bride in the receiving line (optional).
- Sits to left of groom's mother at parents' table during reception.

ALONG WITH GROOM'S MOTHER AND/OR GROOM, FINANCIAL RESPONSIBILITIES TYPICALLY INCLUDE:

- Own travel expenses and attire
- Rehearsal dinner
- Wedding gift for bridal couple
- Bride's wedding ring
- Gifts for groom's attendants
- Medical exam for groom including blood test
- Bride's bouquet and going away corsage
- Mothers' and grandmothers' corsages
- All boutonnieres
- Officiant's fee
- Marriage license
- Honeymoon expenses

CHRISTIAN CEREMONY FORMATIONS

Processional

Recessional

Altar Line Up

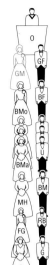

Bride's Pews   Groom's Pews

ABBREVIATIONS

B = Bride
G = Groom
BM = Best Man
MH = Maid of Honor
BF = Bride's Father
BMo = Bride's Mother

GF = Groom's Father
GM = Groom's Mother
BMa = Bridesmaids
U = Ushers
FG = Flower Girl
RB = Ring Bearer
O = Officiant

CHRISTIAN CEREMONY FORMATIONS

Processional

Recessional

Altar Line Up

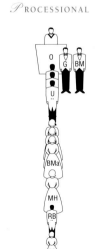
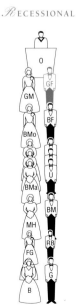

Bride's Pews   Groom's Pews

ABBREVIATIONS

B = Bride
G = Groom
BM = Best Man
MH = Maid of Honor
BF = Bride's Father
BMo = Bride's Mother

GF = Groom's Father
GM = Groom's Mother
BMa = Bridesmaids
U = Ushers
FG = Flower Girl
RB = Ring Bearer
O = Officiant

FLOWER GIRL

- Usually between the ages of four and eight.
- Attends rehearsal to practice her role but is not required to attend pre-wedding parties.
- Arrives dressed at ceremony site 45 minutes before the wedding for photographs.
- Carries a basket filled with loose rose petals to strew along bride's path during processional, if allowed by ceremony site.
- Follows ring bearer or maid of honor and precedes bride during the processional.
- Stands behind maid of honor during ceremony, facing the officiant.

- If very young, may sit with her parents during ceremony.
- Walks beside ring bearer, to his right, immediately following bride and groom during the recessional.
- Sits with her parents during the reception.

HER FAMILY'S FINANCIAL RESPONSIBILITIES TYPICALLY INCLUDE:

- Flower girl's attire except flowers and flower basket
- Travel expenses

RING BEARER

- Usually between the ages of four and eight.
- Attends rehearsal to practice his role but is not required to attend pre-wedding parties.
- Arrives at ceremony site 45 minutes before the wedding for photographs.
- Carries a white pillow with rings attached.
- If younger than 7 years, carries artificial rings.
- Follows maid of honor and precedes flower girl or bride during the processional.
- Stands behind best man during the ceremony, facing the officiant.
- If very young, may sit with his parents during ceremony.

- After the ceremony, carries ring pillow upside down so artificial rings will not show.
- Walks beside flower girl, to her left, immediately following bride and groom during the recessional.
- Sits with his parents during the reception.

HIS FAMILY'S FINANCIAL RESPONSIBILITIES TYPICALLY INCLUDE:

- Ring bearer's attire except ring pillow
- Travel expenses

CHRISTIAN CEREMONY FORMATIONS

Processional

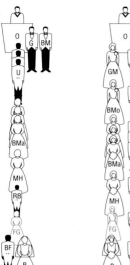

Recessional

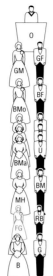

Altar Line Up

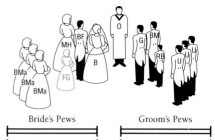

Bride's Pews

Groom's Pews

ABBREVIATIONS

B = Bride	GF = Groom's Father
G = Groom	GM = Groom's Mother
BM = Best Man	BMa = Bridesmaids
MH = Maid of Honor	U = Ushers
BF = Bride's Father	FG = Flower Girl
BMo = Bride's Mother	RB = Ring Bearer
	O = Officiant

CHRISTIAN CEREMONY FORMATIONS

Processional

Recessional

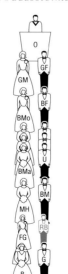

Altar Line Up

Bride's Pews

Groom's Pews

ABBREVIATIONS

B = Bride	GF = Groom's Father
G = Groom	GM = Groom's Mother
BM = Best Man	BMa = Bridesmaids
MH = Maid of Honor	U = Ushers
BF = Bride's Father	FG = Flower Girl
BMo = Bride's Mother	RB = Ring Bearer
	O = Officiant

TRADITIONAL RESPONSIBILITIES

BRIDE

THINGS TO BRING TO REHEARSAL:

- Wedding announcements (for maid of honor to mail after the wedding)
- Bridesmaids' gifts (if not already given)
- Camera and film
- Fake bouquet or ribbon bouquet from bridal shower
- Groom's gift
- Reception maps
- Rehearsal information and lineup chart
- Seating diagrams for head table and parents' tables
- Wedding schedule of events/timeline
- Wedding programs
- Tape player with wedding music

THINGS TO BRING TO WEDDING:

- Aspirin/Alka Seltzer
- Bobby pins
- Breath spray/mints
- Bridal gown
- Bridal gown box
- Cake knife
- Change of clothes for going away
- Clear nail polish
- Deodorant
- Garter
- Gloves
- Groom's ring
- Guest book
- Hair brush
- Hair spray
- Head piece
- Jewelry
- Kleenex
- Lint brush
- Luggage
- Make-up
- Mirror
- Nail polish
- Panty hose
- Passport/Visa
- Perfume
- Personal camera
- Plume pen for guest book
- Powder
- Purse
- Safety pins
- Scotch tape/masking tape
- Sewing kit
- Shoes
- Something old
- Something new
- Something borrowed
- Something blue
- Spot remover
- Straight pins
- Steamer
- Tampons or sanitary napkins
- Toasting goblets
- Toothbrush & paste
- Travelers' checks

TRADITIONAL RESPONSIBILITIES

GROOM

THINGS TO BRING TO REHEARSAL:

- Bride's gift
- Marriage license
- Ushers' gifts (if not already given)
- Service providers' fees to give to best man or wedding consultant so s/he can pay them at the wedding

THINGS TO BRING TO WEDDING:

- Airline tickets
- Announcements
- Aspirin/Alka Seltzer
- Breath spray/mints
- Bride's ring
- Change of clothes for going away
- Cologne
- Cuff Links
- Cummerbund
- Deodorant
- Hair comb
- Hair spray
- Kleenex
- Lint brush
- Luggage
- Neck tie
- Passport/Visa
- Shirt
- Shoes
- Socks
- Toothbrush & paste
- Travelers' checks
- Tuxedo

CHRISTIAN CEREMONY FORMATIONS

Processional   *Recessional*   *Altar Line Up*

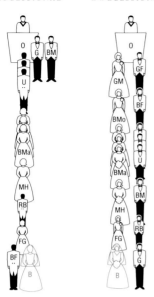

Bride's Pews   Groom's Pews

Abbreviations

B = Bride	GF = Groom's Father
G = Groom	GM = Groom's Mother
BM = Best Man	BMa = Bridesmaids
MH = Maid of Honor	U = Ushers
BF = Bride's Father	FG = Flower Girl
BMo = Bride's Mother	RB = Ring Bearer
	O = Officiant

CHRISTIAN CEREMONY FORMATIONS

Processional   *Recessional*   *Altar Line Up*

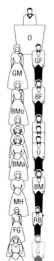

Bride's Pews   Groom's Pews

Abbreviations

B = Bride	GF = Groom's Father
G = Groom	GM = Groom's Mother
BM = Best Man	BMa = Bridesmaids
MH = Maid of Honor	U = Ushers
BF = Bride's Father	FG = Flower Girl
BMo = Bride's Mother	RB = Ring Bearer
	O = Officiant

TRADITIONAL RESPONSIBILITIES

MAID OF HONOR

- Helps bride select attire and address invitations.
- Mails wedding announcements after the wedding if necessary.
- Plans bridal shower for bride.
- Arrives at dressing site 2 hours before ceremony to assist bride in dressing.
- Arrives dressed at ceremony site 1 hour before the wedding for photographs.
- Arranges the bride's veil and train before the processional and recessional.
- Follows bridesmaids and precedes ring bearer/flower girl or bride and her parents during the processional.
- Stands to bride's right under the chuppah.
- Holds bride's bouquet and groom's ring during the ceremony.

- Is escorted out by best man, to his left, immediately following flower girl/ring bearer or groom's parents during the recessional.
- May witness the signing of the marriage certificate, though this is not always possible since conservative and orthodox rabbi's do not let women sign.
- Stands to the left of groom in the receiving line.
- Sits to the left of groom at the head table.
- Keeps bride on schedule.
- Dances with best man during the bridal party dance.
- Helps bride change into her going away clothes.

FINANCIAL RESPONSIBILITIES TYPICALLY INCLUDE:

- Own attire
- Travel expenses
- Accommodations

TRADITIONAL RESPONSIBILITIES

BEST MAN

- Responsible for organizing ushers' activities.
- Organizes bachelor party for groom.
- Drives groom to ceremony site and sees that he is properly dressed before the wedding.
- Arrives dressed at ceremony site 1 hour before the wedding for photographs.
- Brings marriage license to wedding.
- Pays the rabbi, musicians, and any other service providers the day of the wedding.
- Follows ushers and precedes groom and his parents during the processional.
- Stands to groom's left under chuppah.
- Holds the bride's ring for the groom until needed by rabbi.
- Escorts maid of honor, to her right, immediately following flower girl/ring bearer or groom's parents during the recessional.
- May witness the signing of the marriage certificate, though this is not always possible since some rabbi's specify that the witness needs

to be a Jewish male, and not a blood relative to the bride or groom.
- Drives newlyweds to reception if no hired driver.
- Offers first toast at reception, usually before dinner.
- Sits to the right of bride at the head table.
- Keeps groom on schedule.
- Dances with maid of honor during the bridal party dance.
- May drive couple to airport or honeymoon suite.
- Oversees return of tuxedo rentals for groom and ushers, on time and in good condition.

FINANCIAL RESPONSIBILITIES TYPICALLY INCLUDE:

- Own attire
- Travel expenses
- Accommodations

JEWISH CEREMONY FORMATIONS

PROCESSIONAL

RECESSIONAL

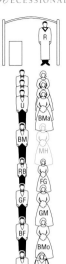

ALTAR LINE UP

Groom's Pews

Bride's Pews

ABBREVIATIONS

B = Bride	GF = Groom's Father
G = Groom	GM = Groom's Mother
BM = Best Man	BMa = Bridesmaids
MH = Maid of Honor	U = Ushers
BF = Bride's Father	FG = Flower Girl
BMo = Bride's Mother	RB = Ring Bearer
	R = Rabbi

JEWISH CEREMONY FORMATIONS

PROCESSIONAL

RECESSIONAL

ALTAR LINE UP

Groom's Pews

Bride's Pews

ABBREVIATIONS

B = Bride	GF = Groom's Father
G = Groom	GM = Groom's Mother
BM = Best Man	BMa = Bridesmaids
MH = Maid of Honor	U = Ushers
BF = Bride's Father	FG = Flower Girl
BMo = Bride's Mother	RB = Ring Bearer
	R = Rabbi

$\mathcal{B}$RIDESMAIDS

- Assist maid/matron of honor in planning bridal shower.
- Assist bride with errands and addressing invitations.
- Participate in all pre-wedding parties.
- Arrive at dressing site 2 hours before ceremony.
- Arrive dressed at ceremony site 1 hour before the wedding for photographs.
- Walk in single file behind groom and his parents in order of height during the processional.
- Stand behind bride's parents during the ceremony, facing the rabbi.
- Are escorted out by ushers (to ushers' left) immediately following maid of honor and best man during recessional.

- Stand to left of maid of honor in receiving line (optional).
- Sit next to ushers at the head table.
- Dance with ushers and other important guests.
- Encourage single women to participate in the bouquet-tossing ceremony.

FINANCIAL RESPONSIBILITIES TYPICALLY INCLUDE:

- Own attire
- Travel expenses
- Accommodations

$\mathcal{B}$RIDESMAIDS

- Assist maid/matron of honor in planning bridal shower.
- Assist bride with errands and addressing invitations.
- Participate in all pre-wedding parties.
- Arrive at dressing site 2 hours before ceremony.
- Arrive dressed at ceremony site 1 hour before the wedding for photographs.
- Walk in single file behind groom and his parents in order of height during the processional.
- Stand behind bride's parents during the ceremony, facing the rabbi.
- Are escorted out by ushers (to ushers' left) immediately following maid of honor and best man during recessional.

- Stand to left of maid of honor in receiving line (optional).
- Sit next to ushers at the head table.
- Dance with ushers and other important guests.
- Encourage single women to participate in the bouquet-tossing ceremony.

FINANCIAL RESPONSIBILITIES TYPICALLY INCLUDE:

- Own attire
- Travel expenses
- Accommodations

PROCESSIONAL

RECESSIONAL

ALTAR LINE UP

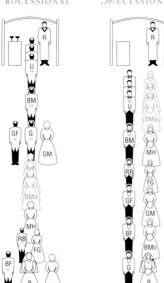

Groom's Pews

Bride's Pews

JEWISH CEREMONY FORMATIONS

PROCESSIONAL

RECESSIONAL

ALTAR LINE UP

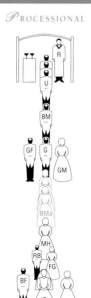

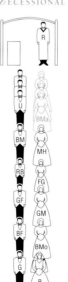

Groom's Pews

Bride's Pews

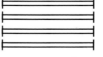

$\mathscr{B}$RIDESMAIDS

- Assist maid/matron of honor in planning bridal shower.
- Assist bride with errands and addressing invitations.
- Participate in all pre-wedding parties.
- Arrive at dressing site 2 hours before ceremony.
- Arrive dressed at ceremony site 1 hour before the wedding for photographs.
- Walk in single file behind groom and his parents in order of height during the processional.
- Stand behind bride's parents during the ceremony, facing the rabbi.
- Are escorted out by ushers (to ushers' left) immediately following maid of honor and best man during recessional.

- Stand to left of maid of honor in receiving line (optional).
- Sit next to ushers at the head table.
- Dance with ushers and other important guests.
- Encourage single women to participate in the bouquet-tossing ceremony.

FINANCIAL RESPONSIBILITIES TYPICALLY INCLUDE:

- Own attire
- Travel expenses
- Accommodations

TRADITIONAL RESPONSIBILITIES

$\mathscr{B}$RIDESMAIDS

- Assist maid/matron of honor in planning bridal shower.
- Assist bride with errands and addressing invitations.
- Participate in all pre-wedding parties.
- Arrive at dressing site 2 hours before ceremony.
- Arrive dressed at ceremony site 1 hour before the wedding for photographs.
- Walk in single file behind groom and his parents in order of height during the processional.
- Stand behind bride's parents during the ceremony, facing the rabbi.
- Are escorted out by ushers (to ushers' left) immediately following maid of honor and best man during recessional.

- Stand to left of maid of honor in receiving line (optional).
- Sit next to ushers at the head table.
- Dance with ushers and other important guests.
- Encourage single women to participate in the bouquet-tossing ceremony.

FINANCIAL RESPONSIBILITIES TYPICALLY INCLUDE:

- Own attire
- Travel expenses
- Accommodations

Processional

Recessional

Altar Line Up

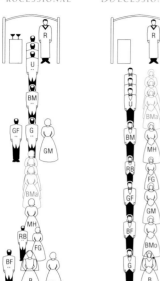

Groom's Pews

Bride's Pews

Abbreviations

B = Bride	GF = Groom's Father
G = Groom	GM = Groom's Mother
BM = Best Man	BMa = Bridesmaids
MH = Maid of Honor	U = Ushers
BF = Bride's Father	FG = Flower Girl
BMo = Bride's Mother	RB = Ring Bearer
	R = Rabbi

JEWISH CEREMONY FORMATIONS

Processional

Recessional

Altar Line Up

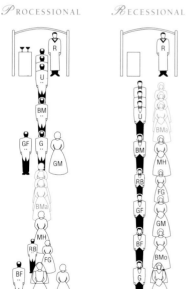

Groom's Pews

Bride's Pews

Abbreviations

B = Bride	GF = Groom's Father
G = Groom	GM = Groom's Mother
BM = Best Man	BMa = Bridesmaids
MH = Maid of Honor	U = Ushers
BF = Bride's Father	FG = Flower Girl
BMo = Bride's Mother	RB = Ring Bearer
	R = Rabbi

*B*RIDESMAIDS

- Assist maid/matron of honor in planning bridal shower.
- Assist bride with errands and addressing invitations.
- Participate in all pre-wedding parties.
- Arrive at dressing site 2 hours before ceremony.
- Arrive dressed at ceremony site 1 hour before the wedding for photographs.
- Walk in single file behind groom and his parents in order of height during the processional.
- Stand behind bride's parents during the ceremony, facing the rabbi.
- Are escorted out by ushers (to ushers' left) immediately following maid of honor and best man during recessional.

- Stand to left of maid of honor in receiving line (optional).
- Sit next to ushers at the head table.
- Dance with ushers and other important guests.
- Encourage single women to participate in the bouquet-tossing ceremony.

FINANCIAL RESPONSIBILITIES TYPICALLY INCLUDE:

- Own attire
- Travel expenses
- Accommodations

TRADITIONAL RESPONSIBILITIES

*B*RIDESMAIDS

- Assist maid/matron of honor in planning bridal shower.
- Assist bride with errands and addressing invitations.
- Participate in all pre-wedding parties.
- Arrive at dressing site 2 hours before ceremony.
- Arrive dressed at ceremony site 1 hour before the wedding for photographs.
- Walk in single file behind groom and his parents in order of height during the processional.
- Stand behind bride's parents during the ceremony, facing the rabbi.
- Are escorted out by ushers (to ushers' left) immediately following maid of honor and best man during recessional.

- Stand to left of maid of honor in receiving line (optional).
- Sit next to ushers at the head table.
- Dance with ushers and other important guests.
- Encourage single women to participate in the bouquet-tossing ceremony.

FINANCIAL RESPONSIBILITIES TYPICALLY INCLUDE:

- Own attire
- Travel expenses
- Accommodations

Processional   *Recessional*   *Altar Line Up*

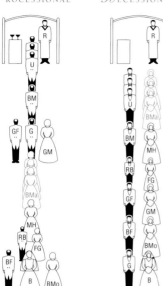

Groom's Pews   Bride's Pews

Abbreviations

B = Bride	GF = Groom's Father
G = Groom	GM = Groom's Mother
BM = Best Man	BMa = Bridesmaids
MH = Maid of Honor	U = Ushers
BF = Bride's Father	FG = Flower Girl
BMo = Bride's Mother	RB = Ring Bearer
	R = Rabbi

JEWISH CEREMONY FORMATIONS

Processional   *Recessional*   *Altar Line Up*

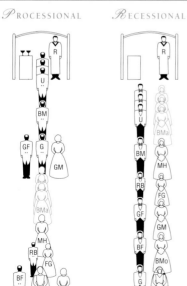

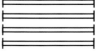

Groom's Pews   Bride's Pews

Abbreviations

B = Bride	GF = Groom's Father
G = Groom	GM = Groom's Mother
BM = Best Man	BMa = Bridesmaids
MH = Maid of Honor	U = Ushers
BF = Bride's Father	FG = Flower Girl
BMo = Bride's Mother	RB = Ring Bearer
	R = Rabbi

TRADITIONAL RESPONSIBILITIES

𝒰SHERS

- Help best man with bachelor party.
- Arrive dressed at ceremony site 1 hour before the wedding for pre-ceremony photographs and to seat guests as they arrive.
- Distribute skull caps and wedding programs to guests as they arrive.
- Seat guests at the ceremony as follows:
  - If female, offer the right arm.
  - If male, walk along his left side.
  - If couple, offer right arm to female; male follows a step or two behind.
  - Seat bride's guests in right pews.
  - Seat groom's guests in left pews.
  - Leave the first several rows of pews open on both sides for seating family members and other VIPs.
  - Maintain equal number of guests in left and right pews, if possible.
  - Should a group of guests arrive at the same time, seat the eldest woman first.
  - Just prior to the processional, escort groom's grandmother to her seat; then escort bride's grandmother to her seat.

- Two ushers may roll carpet down the aisle after both grandmothers are seated.
- Lead the procession in single file, in order of height.
- Stand behind groom's parents during the ceremony, facing the rabbi.
- Escort bridesmaids (to bridesmaids' right) immediately following maid of honor and best man during recessional.
- If pew ribbons are used, two ushers may loosen them one row at a time after the ceremony.
- Keep an eye out for items left in pews.
- Direct guests to the reception site and distribute maps after ceremony.
- Sit at the head table next to bridesmaids.
- Dance with bridesmaids and other important guests.
- Encourage single men to participate in the garter ceremony.

FINANCIAL RESPONSIBILITIES TYPICALLY INCLUDE:

- Own attire
- Travel expenses
- Accommodations

TRADITIONAL RESPONSIBILITIES

𝒰SHERS

- Help best man with bachelor party.
- Arrive dressed at ceremony site 1 hour before the wedding for pre-ceremony photographs and to seat guests as they arrive.
- Distribute skull caps and wedding programs to guests as they arrive.
- Seat guests at the ceremony as follows:
  - If female, offer the right arm.
  - If male, walk along his left side.
  - If couple, offer right arm to female; male follows a step or two behind.
  - Seat bride's guests in right pews.
  - Seat groom's guests in left pews.
  - Leave the first several rows of pews open on both sides for seating family members and other VIPs.
  - Maintain equal number of guests in left and right pews, if possible.
  - Should a group of guests arrive at the same time, seat the eldest woman first.
  - Just prior to the processional, escort groom's grandmother to her seat; then escort bride's grandmother to her seat.

- Two ushers may roll carpet down the aisle after both grandmothers are seated.
- Lead the procession in single file, in order of height.
- Stand behind groom's parents during the ceremony, facing the rabbi.
- Escort bridesmaids (to bridesmaids' right) immediately following maid of honor and best man during recessional.
- If pew ribbons are used, two ushers may loosen them one row at a time after the ceremony.
- Keep an eye out for items left in pews.
- Direct guests to the reception site and distribute maps after ceremony.
- Sit at the head table next to bridesmaids.
- Dance with bridesmaids and other important guests.
- Encourage single men to participate in the garter ceremony.

FINANCIAL RESPONSIBILITIES TYPICALLY INCLUDE:

- Own attire
- Travel expenses
- Accommodations

PROCESSIONAL   RECESSIONAL   ALTAR LINE UP

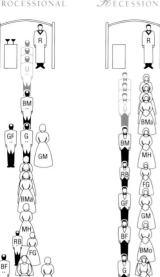

Groom's Pews   Bride's Pews

ABBREVIATIONS

B = Bride   GF = Groom's Father
G = Groom   GM = Groom's Mother
BM = Best Man   BMa = Bridesmaids
MH = Maid of Honor   U = Ushers
BF = Bride's Father   FG = Flower Girl
BMo = Bride's Mother   RB = Ring Bearer
                             R = Rabbi

JEWISH CEREMONY FORMATIONS

PROCESSIONAL   RECESSIONAL   ALTAR LINE UP

Groom's Pews   Bride's Pews

ABBREVIATIONS

B = Bride   GF = Groom's Father
G = Groom   GM = Groom's Mother
BM = Best Man   BMa = Bridesmaids
MH = Maid of Honor   U = Ushers
BF = Bride's Father   FG = Flower Girl
BMo = Bride's Mother   RB = Ring Bearer
                             R = Rabbi

U SHERS

- Help best man with bachelor party.
- Arrive dressed at ceremony site 1 hour before the wedding for pre-ceremony photographs and to seat guests as they arrive.
- Distribute skull caps and wedding programs to guests as they arrive.
- Seat guests at the ceremony as follows:
  - If female, offer the right arm.
  - If male, walk along his left side.
  - If couple, offer right arm to female; male follows a step or two behind.
  - Seat bride's guests in right pews.
  - Seat groom's guests in left pews.
  - Leave the first several rows of pews open on both sides for seating family members and other VIPs.
  - Maintain equal number of guests in left and right pews, if possible.
  - Should a group of guests arrive at the same time, seat the eldest woman first.
  - Just prior to the processional, escort groom's grandmother to her seat; then escort bride's grandmother to her seat.

- Two ushers may roll carpet down the aisle after both grandmothers are seated.
- Lead the procession in single file, in order of height.
- Stand behind groom's parents during the ceremony, facing the rabbi.
- Escort bridesmaids (to bridesmaids' right) immediately following maid of honor and best man during recessional.
- If pew ribbons are used, two ushers may loosen them one row at a time after the ceremony.
- Keep an eye out for items left in pews.
- Direct guests to the reception site and distribute maps after ceremony.
- Sit at the head table next to bridesmaids.
- Dance with bridesmaids and other important guests.
- Encourage single men to participate in the garter ceremony.

FINANCIAL RESPONSIBILITIES TYPICALLY INCLUDE:

- Own attire
- Travel expenses
- Accommodations

TRADITIONAL RESPONSIBILITIES

U SHERS

- Help best man with bachelor party.
- Arrive dressed at ceremony site 1 hour before the wedding for pre-ceremony photographs and to seat guests as they arrive.
- Distribute skull caps and wedding programs to guests as they arrive.
- Seat guests at the ceremony as follows:
  - If female, offer the right arm.
  - If male, walk along his left side.
  - If couple, offer right arm to female; male follows a step or two behind.
  - Seat bride's guests in right pews.
  - Seat groom's guests in left pews.
  - Leave the first several rows of pews open on both sides for seating family members and other VIPs.
  - Maintain equal number of guests in left and right pews, if possible.
  - Should a group of guests arrive at the same time, seat the eldest woman first.
  - Just prior to the processional, escort groom's grandmother to her seat; then escort bride's grandmother to her seat.

- Two ushers may roll carpet down the aisle after both grandmothers are seated.
- Lead the procession in single file, in order of height.
- Stand behind groom's parents during the ceremony, facing the rabbi.
- Escort bridesmaids (to bridesmaids' right) immediately following maid of honor and best man during recessional.
- If pew ribbons are used, two ushers may loosen them one row at a time after the ceremony.
- Keep an eye out for items left in pews.
- Direct guests to the reception site and distribute maps after ceremony.
- Sit at the head table next to bridesmaids.
- Dance with bridesmaids and other important guests.
- Encourage single men to participate in the garter ceremony.

FINANCIAL RESPONSIBILITIES TYPICALLY INCLUDE:

- Own attire
- Travel expenses
- Accommodations

JEWISH CEREMONY FORMATIONS

PROCESSIONAL   RECESSIONAL

ALTAR LINE UP

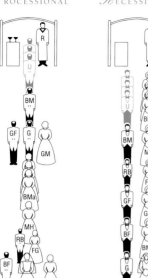

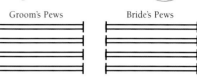

Groom's Pews

Bride's Pews

ABBREVIATIONS

B = Bride	GF = Groom's Father
G = Groom	GM = Groom's Mother
BM = Best Man	BMa = Bridesmaids
MH = Maid of Honor	U = Ushers
BF = Bride's Father	FG = Flower Girl
BMo = Bride's Mother	RB = Ring Bearer
	R = Rabbi

JEWISH CEREMONY FORMATIONS

PROCESSIONAL   RECESSIONAL

ALTAR LINE UP

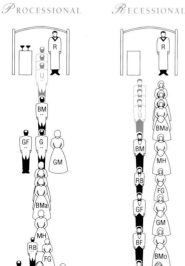

Groom's Pews

Bride's Pews

ABBREVIATIONS

B = Bride	GF = Groom's Father
G = Groom	GM = Groom's Mother
BM = Best Man	BMa = Bridesmaids
MH = Maid of Honor	U = Ushers
BF = Bride's Father	FG = Flower Girl
BMo = Bride's Mother	RB = Ring Bearer
	R = Rabbi

TRADITIONAL RESPONSIBILITIES

*U*SHERS

- Help best man with bachelor party.
- Arrive dressed at ceremony site 1 hour before the wedding for pre-ceremony photographs and to seat guests as they arrive.
- Distribute skull caps and wedding programs to guests as they arrive.
- Seat guests at the ceremony as follows:
  - If female, offer the right arm.
  - If male, walk along his left side.
  - If couple, offer right arm to female; male follows a step or two behind.
  - Seat bride's guests in right pews.
  - Seat groom's guests in left pews.
  - Leave the first several rows of pews open on both sides for seating family members and other VIPs.
  - Maintain equal number of guests in left and right pews, if possible.
  - Should a group of guests arrive at the same time, seat the eldest woman first.
  - Just prior to the processional, escort groom's grandmother to her seat; then escort bride's grandmother to her seat.

- Two ushers may roll carpet down the aisle after both grandmothers are seated.
- Lead the procession in single file, in order of height.
- Stand behind groom's parents during the ceremony, facing the rabbi.
- Escort bridesmaids (to bridesmaids' right) immediately following maid of honor and best man during recessional.
- If pew ribbons are used, two ushers may loosen them one row at a time after the ceremony.
- Keep an eye out for items left in pews.
- Direct guests to the reception site and distribute maps after ceremony.
- Sit at the head table next to bridesmaids.
- Dance with bridesmaids and other important guests.
- Encourage single men to participate in the garter ceremony.

FINANCIAL RESPONSIBILITIES TYPICALLY INCLUDE:
- Own attire
- Travel expenses
- Accommodations

TRADITIONAL RESPONSIBILITIES

*U*SHERS

- Help best man with bachelor party.
- Arrive dressed at ceremony site 1 hour before the wedding for pre-ceremony photographs and to seat guests as they arrive.
- Distribute skull caps and wedding programs to guests as they arrive.
- Seat guests at the ceremony as follows:
  - If female, offer the right arm.
  - If male, walk along his left side.
  - If couple, offer right arm to female; male follows a step or two behind.
  - Seat bride's guests in right pews.
  - Seat groom's guests in left pews.
  - Leave the first several rows of pews open on both sides for seating family members and other VIPs.
  - Maintain equal number of guests in left and right pews, if possible.
  - Should a group of guests arrive at the same time, seat the eldest woman first.
  - Just prior to the processional, escort groom's grandmother to her seat; then escort bride's grandmother to her seat.

- Two ushers may roll carpet down the aisle after both grandmothers are seated.
- Lead the procession in single file, in order of height.
- Stand behind groom's parents during the ceremony, facing the rabbi.
- Escort bridesmaids (to bridesmaids' right) immediately following maid of honor and best man during recessional.
- If pew ribbons are used, two ushers may loosen them one row at a time after the ceremony.
- Keep an eye out for items left in pews.
- Direct guests to the reception site and distribute maps after ceremony.
- Sit at the head table next to bridesmaids.
- Dance with bridesmaids and other important guests.
- Encourage single men to participate in the garter ceremony.

FINANCIAL RESPONSIBILITIES TYPICALLY INCLUDE:
- Own attire
- Travel expenses
- Accommodations

JEWISH CEREMONY FORMATIONS

Processional   *Recessional*   *Altar Line Up*

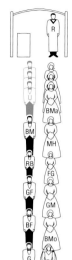

Groom's Pews

Bride's Pews

Abbreviations

B = Bride
G = Groom
BM = Best Man
MH = Maid of Honor
BF = Bride's Father
BMo = Bride's Mother

GF = Groom's Father
GM = Groom's Mother
BMa = Bridesmaids
U = Ushers
FG = Flower Girl
RB = Ring Bearer
R = Rabbi

JEWISH CEREMONY FORMATIONS

Processional   *Recessional*   *Altar Line Up*

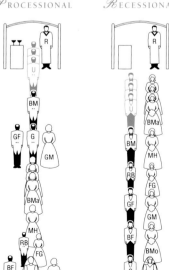

Groom's Pews

Bride's Pews

Abbreviations

B = Bride
G = Groom
BM = Best Man
MH = Maid of Honor
BF = Bride's Father
BMo = Bride's Mother

GF = Groom's Father
GM = Groom's Mother
BMa = Bridesmaids
U = Ushers
FG = Flower Girl
RB = Ring Bearer
R = Rabbi

TRADITIONAL RESPONSIBILITIES

MOTHER OF THE BRIDE

- Helps prepare guest list for bride and her family.
- Helps plan the wedding ceremony and reception.
- Helps bride select her bridal gown.
- Helps bride keep track of gifts received.
- Selects her own attire according to the formality and color of the wedding.
- Makes accommodations for bride's out of town guests.
- Rides to ceremony with bride and her father in limousine.
- Arrives dressed at ceremony site 1 hour before the wedding for photographs.
- Escorts the bride down the aisle (to bride's right), immediately following flower girl/ring bearer or maid of honor during the processional.
- Stands to the right of maid of honor during the ceremony.
- May stand beneath the chuppah during the ceremony, along with the bride and groom and honor attendants.
- Is escorted out by bride's father, to his left, immediately following the bride and groom during the recessional.
- Stands at the head of the receiving line.
- Sits to the right of bride's father at parents' table during reception.
- Dances with the groom after the first dance.
- Acts as hostess at the reception.

ALONG WITH BRIDE'S FATHER AND/OR BRIDE, FINANCIAL RESPONSIBILITIES TYPICALLY INCLUDE:

- Engagement party
- Wedding consultant's fee
- Bridal gown, veil and accessories
- Wedding stationery, calligraphy and postage
- Wedding gift for bridal couple
- Groom's wedding ring
- Gifts for bridesmaids
- Pre-wedding parties and bridesmaids' luncheon
- Photography and videography
- Bride's medical exam and blood test
- Wedding guest book and other accessories
- Rental fee for ceremony site including flowers, music and accessories
- Total cost of reception including rental fees, food, beverages, music, cake, flowers, decorations, favors, etc.
- Transportation for bridal party to ceremony and reception
- Own attire and travel expenses

TRADITIONAL RESPONSIBILITIES

FATHER OF THE BRIDE

- Helps prepare guest list for bride and her family.
- Selects attire that complements groom's attire.
- Rides to the ceremony with bride and her mother in limousine.
- Arrives dressed at ceremony site 1 hour before the wedding for photographs.
- Escorts the bride down the aisle, to her left, immediately following ring bearer/flower girl or maid of honor during the processional.
- Stands to the right of bride's mother during the ceremony.
- May stand beneath the chuppah during the ceremony, along with the bride and groom and honor attendants.
- Escorts bride's mother, to her right, immediately following bride and groom during the recessional.
- Stands to the left of bride's mother in the receiving line (optional).
- Sits to the left of bride's mother at parents' table during reception.
- Dances with bride after first dance.
- Acts as host at the reception.

ALONG WITH BRIDE'S MOTHER AND/OR BRIDE, FINANCIAL RESPONSIBILITIES TYPICALLY INCLUDE:

- Engagement party
- Wedding consultant's fee
- Bridal gown, veil and accessories
- Wedding stationery, calligraphy and postage
- Wedding gift for bridal couple
- Groom's wedding ring
- Gifts for bridesmaids
- Pre-wedding parties and bridesmaids' luncheon
- Photography and videography
- Bride's medical exam and blood test
- Wedding guest book and other accessories
- Total cost of ceremony including flowers, music rental fees and accessories.
- Total cost of reception including rental fees, food, beverages, music, cake, flowers, decorations, favors, etc.
- Transportation for bridal party to ceremony and reception
- Own attire and travel expenses

JEWISH CEREMONY FORMATIONS

Processional

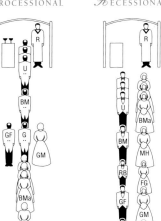

Recessional

Altar Line Up

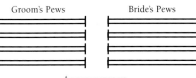

Groom's Pews

Bride's Pews

Abbreviations

B = Bride
G = Groom
BM = Best Man
MH = Maid of Honor
BF = Bride's Father
BMo = Bride's Mother

GF = Groom's Father
GM = Groom's Mother
BMa = Bridesmaids
U = Ushers
FG = Flower Girl
RB = Ring Bearer
R = Rabbi

JEWISH CEREMONY FORMATIONS

Processional

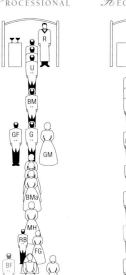

Recessional

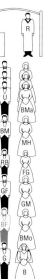

Altar Line Up

Groom's Pews

Bride's Pews

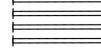

Abbreviations

B = Bride
G = Groom
BM = Best Man
MH = Maid of Honor
BF = Bride's Father
BMo = Bride's Mother

GF = Groom's Father
GM = Groom's Mother
BMa = Bridesmaids
U = Ushers
FG = Flower Girl
RB = Ring Bearer
R = Rabbi

MOTHER OF THE GROOM

- Helps prepare guest list for groom and his family.
- Selects attire that complements mother of the bride's attire.
- Makes accommodations for groom's out of town guests.
- With groom's father, plans rehearsal dinner.
- Arrives dressed at ceremony site 1 hour before the wedding for photographs.
- Escorts the groom down the aisle, to his right, immediately following the best man during the processional.
- Stands to the left of best man during the ceremony.
- May stand beneath the chuppah during the ceremony, along with the bride and groom and honor attendants.
- Is escorted out by groom's father, to his left, immediately following bride's parents during the recessional.
- Stands to the left of bride's parents in the receiving line.
- Sits to the right of groom's father at parents' table during reception.

ALONG WITH GROOM'S FATHER AND/OR GROOM, FINANCIAL RESPONSIBILITIES TYPICALLY INCLUDE:

- Own travel expenses and attire
- Rehearsal dinner
- Wedding gift for bridal couple
- Bride's wedding ring
- Gifts for groom's attendants
- Medical exam for groom including blood test
- Bride's bouquet and going away corsage
- Mothers' and grandmothers' corsages
- All boutonnieres
- Rabbi's fee
- Marriage license
- Honeymoon expenses

FATHER OF THE GROOM

- Helps prepare guest list for groom and his family.
- Selects attire that complements groom's attire.
- With groom's mother, plans rehearsal dinner.
- Offers toast to bride at rehearsal dinner.
- Arrives dressed at ceremony site 1 hour before the wedding for photographs.
- Escorts the groom down the aisle (to groom's left), immediately following the best man during the processional.
- Stands to the left of groom's mother during the ceremony.
- May stand beneath the chuppah during the ceremony, along with the bride and groom and honor attendants.
- Escorts groom's mother, to her right, immediately following bride's parents during the recessional.
- Stands to the left of the groom's mother and to the right of the bride in the receiving line (optional).
- Sits to left of groom's mother at parents' table during reception.

ALONG WITH GROOM'S MOTHER AND/OR GROOM, FINANCIAL RESPONSIBILITIES TYPICALLY INCLUDE:

- Own travel expenses and attire
- Rehearsal dinner
- Wedding gift for bridal couple
- Bride's wedding ring
- Gifts for groom's attendants
- Medical exam for groom including blood test
- Bride's bouquet and going away corsage
- Mothers' and grandmothers' corsages
- All boutonnieres
- Rabbi's fee
- Marriage license
- Honeymoon expenses

JEWISH CEREMONY FORMATIONS

Processional *Recessional* *Altar Line Up*

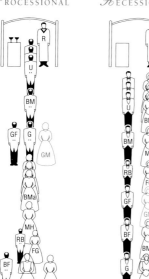

Groom's Pews   Bride's Pews

ABBREVIATIONS

B = Bride	GF = Groom's Father
G = Groom	GM = Groom's Mother
BM = Best Man	BMa = Bridesmaids
MH = Maid of Honor	U = Ushers
BF = Bride's Father	FG = Flower Girl
BMo = Bride's Mother	RB = Ring Bearer
	R = Rabbi

JEWISH CEREMONY FORMATIONS

Processional *Recessional* *Altar Line Up*

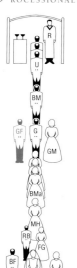

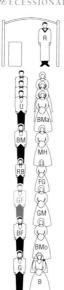

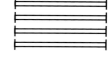

Groom's Pews   Bride's Pews

ABBREVIATIONS

B = Bride	GF = Groom's Father
G = Groom	GM = Groom's Mother
BM = Best Man	BMa = Bridesmaids
MH = Maid of Honor	U = Ushers
BF = Bride's Father	FG = Flower Girl
BMo = Bride's Mother	RB = Ring Bearer
	R = Rabbi

FLOWER GIRL

- Usually between the ages of four and eight.
- Attends rehearsal to practice her role but is not required to attend pre-wedding parties.
- Arrives dressed at ceremony site 45 minutes before the wedding for photographs.
- Carries a basket filled with loose rose petals to strew along bride's path during processional, if allowed by ceremony site.
- Walks to the right of ring bearer, immediately following the maid of honor during the processional.
- Sits with her parents during the ceremony.
- Walks to the left of ring bearer, immediately following groom's parents during the recessional.
- Sits with her parents during the reception.

HER FAMILY'S FINANCIAL RESPONSIBILITIES TYPICALLY INCLUDE:

- Flower girl's attire except flowers and flower basket
- Travel expenses
- Accommodations

RING BEARER

- Usually between the ages of four and eight.
- Attends rehearsal to practice his role but is not required to attend pre-wedding parties.
- Arrives at ceremony site 45 minutes before the wedding for photographs.
- Carries a white pillow with rings attached.
- If younger than 7 years, carries artificial rings.
- Walks to the left of the flower girl, immediately following the maid of honor during the processional.
- Sits with his parents during the ceremony.
- After the ceremony, carries ring pillow upside down so artificial rings will not show.
- Walks to the right of flower girl, immediately following groom's parents during the recessional.
- Sits with his parents during the reception.

HIS FAMILY'S FINANCIAL RESPONSIBILITIES TYPICALLY INCLUDE:

- Ring bearer's attire except ring pillow
- Travel expenses
- Accommodations

JEWISH CEREMONY FORMATIONS

𝒫ROCESSIONAL

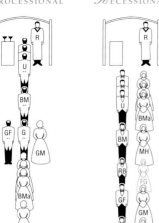

ℛECESSIONAL

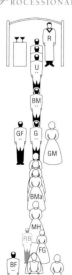

𝒜LTAR 𝓛INE 𝒰P

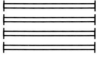 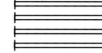

Groom's Pews

Bride's Pews

ABBREVIATIONS

B = Bride	GF = Groom's Father
G = Groom	GM = Groom's Mother
BM = Best Man	BMa = Bridesmaids
MH = Maid of Honor	U = Ushers
BF = Bride's Father	FG = Flower Girl
BMo = Bride's Mother	RB = Ring Bearer
	R = Rabbi

JEWISH CEREMONY FORMATIONS

𝒫ROCESSIONAL

ℛECESSIONAL

𝒜LTAR 𝓛INE 𝒰P

 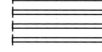

Groom's Pews

Bride's Pews

ABBREVIATIONS

B = Bride	GF = Groom's Father
G = Groom	GM = Groom's Mother
BM = Best Man	BMa = Bridesmaids
MH = Maid of Honor	U = Ushers
BF = Bride's Father	FG = Flower Girl
BMo = Bride's Mother	RB = Ring Bearer
	R = Rabbi

TRADITIONAL RESPONSIBILITIES

ℬRIDE

THINGS TO BRING TO REHEARSAL:

- Wedding announcements (for maid of honor to mail after the wedding)
- Bridesmaids' gifts (if not already given)
- Camera and film
- Fake bouquet or ribbon bouquet from bridal shower
- Groom's gift
- Reception maps
- Rehearsal information and lineup chart
- Seating diagrams for head table and parents' tables
- Wedding schedule of events/timeline
- Wedding programs
- Tape player with wedding music
- Ring bearer's pillow
- Flower girl's basket with petals

THINGS TO BRING TO WEDDING:

- Aspirin/Alka Seltzer
- Bobby pins
- Breath spray/mints
- Bridal gown
- Bridal gown box

- Cake knife
- Change of clothes for going away
- Clear nail polish
- Deodorant
- Garter
- Gloves
- Groom's ring
- Guest book
- Hair brush
- Hair spray
- Head piece
- Jewelry
- Kleenex
- Lint brush
- Luggage
- Make-up
- Mirror
- Nail polish
- Panty hose
- Passport/Visa
- Perfume

- Personal camera
- Plume pen for guest book
- Powder
- Purse
- Safety pins
- Scotch tape/ masking tape
- Sewing kit
- Shoes
- Something old
- Something new
- Something borrowed
- Something blue
- Spot remover
- Straight pins
- Steamer
- Tampons or sanitary napkins
- Toasting goblets
- Toothbrush & paste
- Travelers' Checks

TRADITIONAL RESPONSIBILITIES

𝒢ROOM

THINGS TO BRING TO REHEARSAL:

- Bride's gift
- Marriage license
- Ushers' gifts (if not already given)
- Service providers' fees to give to best man or wedding consultant so s/he can pay them at the wedding

THINGS TO BRING TO WEDDING:

- Airline tickets
- Announcements
- Aspirin/Alka Seltzer
- Breath spray/mints
- Bride's ring
- Change of clothes for going away
- Cologne
- Cuff Links

- Cummerbund
- Deodorant
- Hair comb
- Hair spray
- Kleenex
- Lint brush
- Luggage
- Neck tie
- Passport/Visa
- Shirt
- Shoes
- Socks
- Toothbrush & paste
- Travelers' Checks
- Tuxedo

JEWISH CEREMONY FORMATIONS

PROCESSIONAL

RECESSIONAL

ALTAR LINE UP

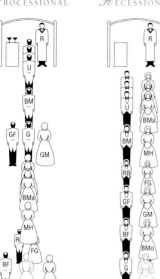

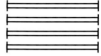

Groom's Pews

Bride's Pews

ABBREVIATIONS

B = Bride	GF = Groom's Father
G = Groom	GM = Groom's Mother
BM = Best Man	BMa = Bridesmaids
MH = Maid of Honor	U = Ushers
BF = Bride's Father	FG = Flower Girl
BMo = Bride's Mother	RB = Ring Bearer
	R = Rabbi

JEWISH CEREMONY FORMATIONS

PROCESSIONAL

RECESSIONAL

ALTAR LINE UP

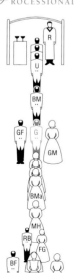

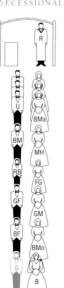

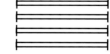

Groom's Pews

Bride's Pews

ABBREVIATIONS

B = Bride	GF = Groom's Father
G = Groom	GM = Groom's Mother
BM = Best Man	BMa = Bridesmaids
MH = Maid of Honor	U = Ushers
BF = Bride's Father	FG = Flower Girl
BMo = Bride's Mother	RB = Ring Bearer
	R = Rabbi